ti

Recording the vision. Making it plain. That you may run.

Dedicated to my beloved family

Foundation
U N I V E R S I T Y   P R E S S

Understanding Japan
Through the Eyes of Christian Faith

Fifth Edition
ISBN: 978-94-90179-18-2
also available as e-book

Foundation University Press
Post Office Box 12429 ǀ 1100 AK Amsterdam ǀ The Netherlands

foundationuniversitypress.com   *book design* ǀ **timmyroland**.com

"My people would not immediately become Christians, but they would first ask you a multitude of questions, weighing carefully your answers and your claims. Above all, they would observe whether your conduct agrees with your words. If you should satisfy them on these points by suitable replies to their inquiries and by a life above reproach, then, as soon as the matter was known and fully examined, the king, the nobles, and the educated people would become Christians. Six months would suffice; for the nation is one that always follows the guidance of reason."

Anjiro, 1548

In 1597, the blood of martyrs was shed on the hills of Nagasaki. This incident is very impressive. Before being executed with 25 other Christians, Ludvico Ibaragi, a 12 year old boy, told an officer who begged him to recant his faith, 'Sir, it would be better if you yourself became a Christian and could go to heaven where I am going. Sir, which is my cross?'

I can sense through this book that Dr. Samuel Lee has a deep concern for Japan and the Japanese people that springs from God's love. He does not have a stereotyped view of Japan. He acknowledges the elements in Japanese culture that hinder Japanese believers from sharing the gospel with others. He indicates that gumi consisted of five or more households and that members were obligated to report any hidden Christians to the authorities as part of the organized persecution of Christians in the Tokugawa period.

His analysis regarding the Japanese cultural strongholds of the concepts of honne/tatemae and uchi/soto that hinder churches from growing is very insightful and provides us with key strategies for reaching Japan with the gospel. He reveals sociocultural disorders such as the high suicide rate, hikikomori, and freeter and the challenges facing churches in Japan to acknowledge them and provide means for overcoming these problems.

Samuel Lee challenges us to provide biblical and ethical solutions for Japanese men and women who are experiencing radical social, economical, and cultural changes and who are searching for new answers. After reading this book, I could not help but resolve to rededicate myself to give them the answer by showing them the living and loving Father, for whom Ludvico Ibaragi gave his life. I pray that this book will be a great stimulus to Japanese churches to break down cultural strongholds and reach suffering people with the gospel as never before.

Pastor Hiroko Ayabe
Founder of Japan Revival Ministries
Tama Gospel Center

"I highly recommend this insightful new book from Samuel Lee. He accurately assesses the major cultural and historical barriers to Christianity that have been built into Japanese society, and offers thoughtful strategies for breaking those barriers down. This book will be an asset to anyone who has a heart for Japan and longs to see it transformed."

Rev. Ron Sawka,
President, Christian International Asia
Tochigi, Japan

"Japan is a nation ready for the gospel. However, for decades there has been a missing piece to the missiological puzzle. Samuel Lee's profound book is a giant step toward revealing that missing piece. Once it is uncovered and applied, Japan will experience the bountiful spiritual harvest we have been waiting for!"

C. Peter Wagner, PhD
Chancellor, Wagner Leadership Institute

"Dr. Samuel Lee presents a thorough treatment of Japanese history and society from a Christian perspective. His analysis is helpful for Western Christians who are interested in investigating the factors hindering their effective witness in Japan."

Rev. Mike Wilson
Asian Access, Okinawa, Japan

"Samuel Lee has combined brilliant research and deep spiritual insights to produce a landmark work of scholarship on the spiritual forces that have shaped the nation of Japan. He has made a valuable contribution to the missions' community by unlocking the secrets of a society that has been closed to the rest of the world for centuries. This book provides the global church with a valuable key to opening and reaching Japan with the gospel."

J. Lee Grady
Editor of Charisma from 1999-2010, USA

FIFTH EDITON

Japan has changed, and it has changed a great deal since I wrote the first edition of *Understanding Japan Through the Eyes of Christian Faith* in 2006. It is difficult to keep up with the growing social, political, economic, and spiritual changes in the country. Japan's demographic decline, the increasing number of elderly in comparison to the number of working class, the increase of crimes committed by the elderly, the systematic discrimination against women, and the rise of maternal harassment, *Matahara*, are only a few concerns when we talk about Japan's rapid change. Due to work stress and pressure of long working hours, Japan's productive population is not much interested in intimate relationships with their partners.

Japan is shifting from a collectivist society to a more individualist society. This rise of individualism is creating many cultural and social changes. The morality and worldviews of the Japanese are changing. Individualist choices are also having demographic consequences, such as a serious decline in the birth rate. This declining birth rate affects the role of women in society. In this fifth edition, I have added relevant information regarding these changes in the appropriate chapters. I also have added some relevant information regarding the contribution of Christianity to Japanese society. Lastly, some of the relevant data and statistics from previous editions have been updated in this fifth edition.

In the past years various organizations and individual missionaries have used *Understanding Japan Through the Eyes of Christian Faith*, and my hope is that it will continue to fulfill the purpose for which it was written.

Introduction

The challenge of understanding Japanese culture and society has attracted many scholars who have researched and written about this fascinating nation. There are various theories about Japan and the best methods for analyzing its culture. I have always been intrigued by Japanese culture. I selected Japan as my regional specialization when studying sociology at university in the Netherlands. Whether we are conscious of it or not, Japanese culture is making an impact on global culture. It is advancing rapidly in unique ways, reaching almost every corner of the world. Not only has Japan dominated the global markets with her cars and electronic products, but now she is also conquering the world through her manga culture and animation characters. This latter phenomenon includes games, films, cartoons, and the marketing associated with them. When in a village in South Africa, I was surprised to discover that the children there had been exposed to Japanese cartoons and animations such as *Pokémon* and *Digimon!* Japanese cartoons and animation characters are often influenced by thousands of years of Japanese mythology and culture. They are being transformed and adapted to the 21st century. Japanese society is "superficially" westernized. At times, it appears to be more westernized than the West itself. The Japanese people are excellent in adopting imported lifestyles by making them their own while adding their own cultural elements. A professor in Japanese sociology said, "Japanese people are more American than the Americans themselves."

While Japanese people have widely adopted western lifestyles, only 2% of the population has received the Christian faith. This book is concerned with how Christians can reach Japan more effectively. Missionaries, churches, and evangelistic organizations will all benefit from this book.

Japanese society is on the verge of undergoing new changes. While young people have all they need materially, there are things they lack both spiritually and mentally. There is a high youth suicide rate in Japan. There are websites that assist people, both young and old, to commit suicide. The cause for this despair is loneliness. While everyone is busy with work and life, the children, youth, women, and elderly are being neglected. Japan is a nation with great Christian potential. People are searching and looking for answers. I believe this is the right time for Christianity to be proclaimed in Japan.

The Japanese are a highly productive people. They promoted their products extremely well and rapidly in the years following World War II; how much more will Japanese Christians promote the gospel of Jesus Christ? But why are Japanese Christians unable to effectively spread the Christian faith? One reason is that there are elements in Japanese culture that make it difficult for Japanese believers to openly share the gospel with others. In this book, I explore some of these Japanese cultural elements and try to explain how these elements can be used to advance the gospel in Japan.

When Japan becomes an exporter of Christianity along with its technology and science, the gospel will advance rapidly not just in Asia but throughout the world! We have to motivate and encourage Japanese believers to share their faith. That is why it is critical to invest in Japanese Christianity and to witness effectively to Japanese people. In order to invest in Japan and prepare this nation for the gospel of Christ, we need to understand Japanese culture. This includes their way of thinking, their society, and the functioning of Japan's social structures.

In this book, I examine the cultural elements of Japanese society that are potential cultural gateways for reaching the Japanese for Christ. I also examine the things that hinder the progress of the gospel in this nation.

Further, I discuss the history and present condition of Christianity in Japan as well as the general condition of religion in this country by considering Buddhism, Shinto, and Confucianism. I discuss

Japanese culture as it relates to the gospel. I then explore the various cultural barriers and hindrances to the gospel. Finally, I present some conclusions and future perspectives.

METHODOLOGY

I have referred to various articles, magazines, and books when writing this book. The Internet has also been a great source of information. My research is predominantly based on a thorough literature study in the fields of sociology and culture of Japan, church history, and sociology of religion. Lastly, this book follows the Japanese name order, which puts the family name in front of the given name. Japanese name order is only valid for Japanese names.

Contents

FIFTH **EDITION**

UNDERSTANDING
JAPAN
THROUGH THE EYES OF **CHRISTIAN** FAITH

SAMUEL **LEE**

AMSTERDAM | BERLIN | SINGAPORE | PORTLAND

JAPAN
A **BRIEF** OVERVIEW

PART **ONE**

Chapter One

The Origin of the Japanese People

Japan is a fascinating country in today's world. This ancient country with a population of approximately 125 million people is one of the most important economic powers in Asia and the world. After World War II and her defeat by the Allied Forces, Japan was in ruins. However, within fifty years, Japan has become a leader in economics, technology, the arts, science, sports, and politics.

Other Asian nations, even though they had been victims of Japanese aggression in World War II, still follow the Japanese way of development. How did it start and what is the root of such development? The answer to this complex question may be found in the historical development of Japan, the development of her culture, and the evolution of Japanese society through the various eras. Before examining the historical aspects, some basic information about the geography of Japan is presented.

Japan consists of four main islands and some 3,900 small islands. These collections of islands extend from Soya in the north to the south near Taiwan. The four main islands of Japan are (from north to south) Hokkaido, Honshu, Shikoku, and Kyushu.

Tokyo, the capital city, and some other important cities like Osaka, Kobe, and Yokohama, are on Honshu, the largest island of the Japan archipelago. Nagasaki is situated in Kyushu. Japan is divided into 47 prefectures, which are equivalent to states or provinces in other countries. The closest neighboring countries to Japan are Russia in the north and North and South Korea in the west.

There have been disputes with neighboring countries concerning the territorial boundaries of Japan. These disputed islands include some islands that are claimed by both Japan and Russia and by Japan and Korea.

The earliest Japanese historical period is the Jomon period, which ran from approximately 8000 BC to 300 BC. The Jomon people were remarkable pottery makers. Many believe that they gradually migrated northward. There are various theories and mythological beliefs concerning the origin of the Japanese people. Some believe that the Jomon people were the first inhabitants of Japan. Some link the origin of the Japanese people to the Tungus people of the north. The Tungus people are a Siberian ethnic group who number about 30,000 today. They are subdivided into the Evenki who live in the area from the Yenisei and Ob river basins to the Pacific Ocean and from the Amur River to the Arctic Ocean, and the Lamut who live on the coast of the Okhotsk Sea. The Tungus people are closely related to the Manchus. Before they were brought under Soviet control, the Tungus practiced a shamanistic religion. The Tungus and Tungusic languages are a division of the Altaic subfamily of the Ural–Altaic family of languages that includes the Manchu literary language; they may be related to Mongolic and Turkic languages. Some believe that the Japanese people originate from the Austronesian people from South Asia of whom Indonesians and Filipinos are examples. Others believe that their origin may be a mixture of both the Tungus and Austronesian people. Another intriguing theory is that the Japanese people are descended from one of the lost tribes of Israel. After discussing the mythological origin of Japan, I will discuss this Japanese-Jewish common ancestry theory.

Mythological Origins

"Mythological origins" refers what the Japanese believe to be the formation of Japan as a nation and a people. Since this is a myth, it is not supported by scientific evidence. Yet it is crucial because it certainly has cultural value, which may influence the way the Japanese people look at their nation and themselves. Therefore, I discuss this mythology regarding the formation of Japan.

The myth starts with ground appearing like oil floating on water. The god, Izanagi, and the goddess, Izanami, looked down on the ground from a very high place in the sky to harden the ground and form a good country. The two inserted a long halberd into the sea to harden the ground and to form a country. They stirred it with rolling. The seawater that dripped from the tip of the halberd accumulated fast and became an island.

When they saw this, they were pleased and descended to this island where they got married. After that, they gave birth to other islands (Shikoku, Honshu, Kyushu, etc). The country of Japan was born in this way. After Izanagi married Izanami, they had a son named Susanoo-no-Mikoto (Susanowo) with the daughter named Amaterasu Omikami (Amaterasu). Amaterasu is the Japanese Shinto sun goddess, ruler of the Plain of Heaven, whose name means, "shining heaven" or "she who shines in the heavens." She is the central figure in the Shinto pantheon and the Japanese Imperial Family claims to be descended from her. She is the eldest daughter of Izanagi. She was so bright and radiant that her parents sent her up the Celestial Ladder to heaven where she has ruled ever since. When her brother, Susanowo, the storm god, ravaged the earth, Amaterasu retreated to a cave because her brother was so boisterous. She closed the cave with a large boulder. Her disappearance deprived the world of light and life and demons ruled the earth. The other gods used everything in their power to lure her out, but to no avail. Finally, Uzume succeeded. The laughter of the gods, when they watched her comical and obscene dances, aroused Amaterasu's curiosity. When she emerged from her cave a streak of light escaped. The goddess then saw her own brilliant reflection in a mirror, which Uzume had hung in a nearby tree. When she drew closer for a better look, the gods grabbed her and pulled her out of the cave. She returned to the sky and brought light back into the world. Later, she created rice fields, called inada, where she cultivated rice. She also invented the art of weaving with the loom and taught the people how to cultivate wheat and silkworms.

Amaterasu's main sanctuary is Ise Jingu at Ise on the island of Honshu. Every 20 years, this temple is dismantled and reconstructed in its original form. Amaterasu is represented by a mirror (her body) in the inner sanctum. She is also called Omikami, meaning "illustrious goddess."

The above account indicates that the Japanese people believe (or at least many of them believe) that Japan is a divine nation according to Shintoism. This may influence how they view their nation and how they behave and relate to other cultures. This kind of thinking was promoted in the Meiji period (1868–1912) of Japanese history. I describe this era later.

Japanese-Jewish Common Ancestry Theory

The Japanese-Jewish common ancestry theory (*Nichiyu Dosoron*) claims the Japanese people are descendants of the ten lost tribes of Israel. Arimasa Kubo, a Japanese scholar, considers certain Japanese cultural ceremonies to be evidences for the Japanese-Jewish common ancestry theory. In his blog post "Israelites Came to Ancient Japan"[1] he discusses some of the ceremonies. With his permission, I extract some information from his blog concerning these ceremonies:

1. *Ontosai Festival – Isaac Story*

2. *Crests of Shinto Shrines of Imperial House of Japan – Star of David*

3. *Tokin – Phylacteries*

4. *Omikoshi – Ark of the Covenant*

5. *Shinto Shrine – Tabernacle of Ancient Israel*

6. *Ancient Japanese People and Yahweh (Jehovah) Kubo notes many other interesting similarities, but we do not consider them here, as they are not so relevant to this book.*

Ontosai Festival — Isaac Story

According to Kubo, there is a link between the *Ontosai* festival and the story of Abraham nearly sacrificing his son Isaac before the angel of the Lord stopped him and provided a ram to be sacrificed in Isaac's place. A traditional festival called *Ontosai* is held every year on

---

1- http://www2.biglobe.ne.jp/~remnant/isracame.htm

April 15 at Suwa Taisha, a large Shinto shrine (Shinto is a traditional religion unique to Japan) in Nagano prefecture. This festival has many similarities with the story of Isaac in Genesis 22 in the Bible in which Abraham was about to sacrifice his own son Isaac in the region of Moraiah.

The *Ontosai* festival has been held since ancient times and is considered the most important festival of Suwa Taisha. Next to the shrine, there is a mountain called Mt. Moriya ("Moriya san" in Japanese). The people from the Suwa area call the god of Mt. Moriya "Moriya no kami", which means "the god of Moriya." At the festival, a boy is tied with a rope to a wooden pillar and placed on a bamboo carpet.

A Shinto priest comes to him with a knife, but then a messenger (another priest) arrives and the boy is released. It is reminiscent of how Isaac was released after an angel came to Abraham. 75 deer are sacrificed at this festival; among them, one deer is believed to have split ears and it is believed to be a deer that the god prepared. It may have some connection with the ram that God prepared for Abraham to sacrifice after Isaac had been released. Even in historic times, people considered this custom of deer sacrifice to be strange because animal sacrifice is not a Shinto tradition. People call this festival "the festival of the *Misakuchi* god." *Misakuchi* might be *"mi-isaku-chi"*, where *"mi"* means "great", "Isaku" is probably Isaac (Hebrew name: Yitzhak), and *"chi"* indicates the end of the word. It seems that the people of Suwa deified Isaac, probably due to the influence of idol worshipers. This custom of a boy about to be sacrificed and then released is no longer practiced today, but a ritual involving a wooden pillar, called "oniye bashira", which means "sacrifice pillar", is still celebrated. Crests of Shinto Shrines of the Imperial House of Japan – Star of David.

Ise Jingu in Mie prefecture is a Shinto shrine built for the Imperial House of Japan. Stone street lamps line both sides of the approaches to the shrine. The Jewish Star of David is carved near the top of each lamp. There is also a crest with the Star of David inside the shrine (*Izawa-no-Miya*) at *Ise Jingu*, which has been there since ancient times. In Kyoto prefecture, there is a shrine called *Manai Jinja*, which was the original *Ise Jingu* Shrine. Its crest is also the Star of David, which has been used since ancient times.

Tokin – Phylacteries

Yamabushis are religious men in training. They are unique to Japan. Today, they are considered to belong to Japanese Buddhism. However, Buddhism in China, Korea, and India has no such custom. The custom of *yamabushi* existed in Japan prior to the introduction of Buddhism in the 7th century. A *yamabushi* wears a small, black box, known as a tokin, which is tied to his head by a black cord. He really resembles a Jew wearing a phylactery (black box) on his forehead with a black cord.

Tokin are similar in size to Jewish phylacteries, but they are round and are shaped like flowers. The Jewish phylactery appears to have originated from the forehead plate that was attached to the high priest with a cord (Exodus 28:36–38). It was about 4 cm (1.6 inches) long according to traditional sources. Some scholars say that it was shaped like a flower; if so, it was very similar in shape to the Japanese tokin worn by the *yamabushi*.

Omikoshi – Ark of the Covenant

Arimasa Kubo notes that Japanese *omikoshi*, which are portable shrines transported in festivals on people's shoulders using poles, resemble the ark of God carried by the Jewish priests in ancient Israel.

Shinto Shrine – Tabernacle of Ancient Israel

The tabernacle of God in ancient Israel was divided into two areas: the Holy Place and the Most Holy Place. According to Kubo, Shinto shrines are also divided into two areas that serve similar functions as the two areas in the Jewish tabernacle. Even the rituals performed in Shinto shrines resemble those performed in the tabernacle of ancient Israel. Just like Jewish people in the tabernacle, normal Japanese people are not permitted to enter the Holy Place — only Shinto priests are allowed to enter. Shinto priests enter the "Holy of Holies" only on special occasions; which is the same as the Jewish tabernacle. The "Holy of Holies" of Japanese Shinto shrines is located on the western side of the shrine, which is the same as the Jewish tabernacle. Shinto's "Holy of Holies" is on a higher level than the "Holy Place" and steps connect the two areas. Scholars say that the "Holy of Holies" in the Jewish temple built by King Solomon was also elevated and that there were steps connecting the two areas. There are two lion statues known as *komainu* that sit on both sides of the approach to a Japanese shrines. They are not idols but guards for the shrine. This is also a custom of ancient Israel. There were statues or reliefs of lions in God's temple in Israel and in Solomon's palace (1 Kings 7:36, 10:19). There was absolutely no mention of lions in the early historical records of Japan. Nevertheless, the lion statues have been placed in front of Japanese shrines since ancient times. Scholars have demonstrated that the lion statues located in front of Japanese shrines originated from the Middle East. In addition to the above-mentioned customs, there are other rituals that resemble the rituals of the tabernacle and Kubo describes them in detail.

Ancient Japanese People and Yahweh (Jehovah)

A major difference between Shintoism and Judaism is that Shintoism worships many gods whereas Judaism believes in only one true God. However, the 10 lost tribes of Israel were inclined to idol worship and polytheistic belief. They believed in the true God, Yahweh, but also worshiped Baal, Ashtoreth, Molech, and other pagan gods. According to the Bible, that is why God was angry with the Israelites. In practice, the religion of ancient Israel was not monotheistic because they disobeyed the commands of the Lord. Shinto's polytheistic belief seems to have originated from the polytheistic inclination of ancient Israel. Some Shinto scholars note that the Shinto god, Susanoh, resembles Baal in several aspects and that the Shinto goddess, Amaterasu, resembles Ashtoreth.

Japanese-Jewish Common Ancestry Theory — Conclusions

Clearly, Shintoism is not identical to ancient Judaism, yet there are some similarities that may indicate that the 10 tribes of Israel migrated to the Middle East, Central and Far Asia, and Japan. If this theory is true, Jews entered Japan during the very early stages of the formation of Japan as a nation and of Shinto belief and Japanese culture. According to this hypothesis, Jewish customs and rituals were readily received and adopted during the formation of this new nation and culture. In this way, Shintoism, which was in a developmental stage, would have adopted Jewish customs along with the pagan customs of Baal and other gods. Since Shintoism was a polytheistic belief, there would have been no problems including more gods in its pantheon.

Chapter Two

A Brief History of Japan

The Aristocratic & Feudal Age

As mentioned above, Japanese history is believed to have started about 8,000 BC with the Jomon period. We do not know much about this period besides that the people made pottery.

Chinese chronicles contain the earliest historical reference to the Japanese people. According to these chronicles, Japan was a nation with 100 kingdoms, 30 of which established diplomatic relations with China by sending envoys. These chronicles also state that in the 3rd century AD there was continuous fighting between these kingdoms. A queen called Himiko ruled a kingdom called Yamatai and she gained power over the other kingdoms. The Yamatai kingdom was located in southern Japan and archeological findings confirm that Yamatai was located in Kyushu. The rulers of Yamatai, the Yamato, gained more power and established the imperial line, which claimed to be directly descended from the god Amaterasu.

Society in the Yamato period was already stratified into ruling (*uji*) and serving (*be*) classes. The *be* were specialized groups that provided various services to the *uji* class. The Yamato family initially belonged to the *uji* class before becoming the Imperial Family. The entire *uji* society was then ranked based on closeness to the imperial line. These principles of social and political organization have provided Japan not only with a symbolic centrality and a sense of identity but also with a blueprint for social order that has been utilized through the centuries and is still operative in modern Japanese society. During the Yamato period, Japan was governed based on Chinese political structure and for the first time the country was controlled by civil and criminal law systems. The *be* system was dismantled and farmers became free tenants of the state and received land for their own use (Hendry, 2004).

9

The city of Nara was built as the capital of Japan. A 100 years later, Heiankyo (contemporary Kyoto) became the new capital city of Japan. These periods are known as the Nara (AD 710-94) and Heian periods (AD 794-1191), respectively. The Imperial Family, the Yamato, ruled in both periods. From the establishment of the Yamato in about AD 300 until the end of the Heian period in AD 1191, Japan was strongly influenced by Chinese culture. The arts and culture bloomed and during the first 500 years, poetry and literature flourished. In addition, architecture really took off in the form of Buddhist temples and other buildings.

This high point of Chinese influence on Japan was the acceptance of Buddhism both as a dominant religion and a powerful establishment. This religion was favored by the central Yamato nobility. Therefore, the government sponsored the construction of splendid temples and extravagant Buddhist ceremonies. Buddhism thus became an integral part of aristocratic life both as a religion and as a cultural force (Hall, 1991).

The imperial family gradually lost its political power to the Fujiwara family. Through marriage alliances with the Imperial Family, the Fujiwara gained more influence and Fujiwara rulers and chancellors and a few other influential families ruled the country. These influential families gradually gained control over areas of cultivated land. The direct relationship between farmers and the government was replaced with a relationship between farmers and local superiors who were connected with these influential families. This process brought about the demise of the aristocratic age and initiated the gradual introduction of feudalism to Japan. The Chinese model of bureaucracy lost its significance and the ruling families and the establishment became more concerned with military strength. They developed a code of ethics and rules that gave birth to samurai warriors. These codes and ethics are known as *bushido* — the way of the samurai! Due to civil unrest, a strong military headquarters was established and it gradually gained more political power and influence.

At the end of the 12th century, Yoritomo, a strong military leader became the chief commander of the military force with the title shogun. Ever since, the power of the shogun grew until 1868. The system that had developed since the first shogun caused Japan to be divided into autonomous provinces under the leadership of local shoguns. These local shoguns were known as *shugos* and *jitos*. The farmers who cultivated the land were obligated to provide their superiors—those working under the local shogun—with rice and other products. In exchange, the local shogun would protect the farmers because farmers were often the victims in battles between landlords due to land disputes. This gave rise to the samurai, who were employed by the local shoguns. They had to protect the local shoguns and their properties as well as the farmers. Samurai gained more power during the Tokugawa period (1603-1867).

According to John W. Hall, practices associated with the feudal system did not spread suddenly or uniformly throughout Japan nor was there a sudden break with the imperial system. The introduction of feudal practices associated with the ascension of Samurai into political and economic leadership occurred gradually over many centuries. Historians have customarily divided this period into three distinct periods: the Kamakura period (1185-1333) when military leadership and feudal practice coexisted with those of the Kyoto court; the Muromachi or Ashikaga period (1338-1573) during which samurai took over the remnants of the imperial system of government and eliminated most of the court proprietorships; and the Tokugawa period (1603-1867) when the samurai class stood unchallenged as the countries rulers and increasingly relied on non-feudal means of government (Hall, 1991).

Japan Encounters Europe

In 1543, during the Ashikaga period, Japan had its first contact with Europeans through three Portuguese sailors who were shipwrecked on the island of Tanegashima off the coast of Kyushu. This was the first encounter between two completely different cultures — the Japanese and European cultures. This encounter had two critical consequences for Japan: the introduction of firearms and the introduction of Catholicism through the arrival of the Portuguese Jesuit priest, Francis Xavier. Later, I discuss the development of Catholicism in Japan and the hostility of the Japanese rulers toward this newly introduced faith.

Tokugawa or Edo Period (1603-1868)

The Tokugawa period is one of the most interesting periods in Japanese history. By the end of the 1500s, Japan was a decentralized nation ruled by military overlords and peasant confederations. At the end of the 16th century, Tokugawa Ieyasu, the head of a small group of warriors, put an end to this decentralized Japan. The victory of Tokugawa Ieyasu at the Battle of Sekigahara in 1600 initiated the Tokugawa period, which endured more than 250 years. After the Battle of Sekigahara, Tokugawa established the foundations for an orderly and disciplined society. Tokugawa and his descendants were able to centralize Japan under the leadership of the Shogun. During these 250 years of discipline, Japanese society was stratified into various levels and everyone was required to belong to a certain social level. Confucianism played an important role in this process of classification. The teachings of Confucius provided the standards for living and belief alongside Buddhist teachings in Japan. It was during the Tokugawa period that certain Buddhist and Confucian precepts became the main social and cultural ethic of the Japanese people. These will be discussed in more detail in the next chapter.

Tokugawa Japan was an agricultural society whose economy depended on agricultural products. During this period, Japan had approximately 30 million inhabitants. The population of Japan stagnated in the 1700s due to urbanization, improved living standards, an increasingly consumption-oriented lifestyle, and urban activities such as the arts. Later, various famines caused food shortages because of antiquated agricultural methods and relatively rapid population growth. The farmers' tax increased and due to a long period of peace starting from 1620, the samurai class gradually (toward the end of this period) lost its military power while still maintaining its symbolic status. Some samurai chose to become farmers and some worked as administrators. During this period, the Emperor still existed but he had almost no power; the country was simply ruled by local shoguns, *shugos,* and *jitos.*

In the Tokugawa period, warlords or *daimyo* ruled the provinces. There were somewhere between 254 and 295 *daimyo.* There were generally three kinds of *daimyo*: collateral *daimyo* (*shinpan*), hereditary *daimyo* (*fudai*), and outer *daimyo* (*tozama*). Those in the first group were relatives or descendants of the first Tokugawa shogun, Tokugawa Ieyasu. The second group was quite close to the shogun, whereas the last group was never offered any central position or office during the Tokugawa period (Lande, 1989).

The encounter with the West and the introduction of Catholicism did not impress the Tokugawa since they considered Europeans and their religion to be a threat. Therefore, they adopted an isolation policy and closed Japan's doors to Westerners (except for the Dutch) for more than 200 years. Why did Japan choose to maintain ties with the Dutch and not with the Portuguese and the Spaniards? We have to realize that at the end of the 16th century and the beginning of the 17th century Japan was somewhat open to foreign powers. Contact with the Portuguese and the Spanish and some trade with South Asian countries like the Philippines and India made Japan aware of the colonial ambitions of Spain and Portugal in the region. The political ambitions of these Latin European nations were accompanied with their desire to spread Catholicism throughout the world, including Japan. This was directed by another religious /political power established in Rome—the Vatican.

The Dutch, however, were just emerging as a colonial nation and were the enemy of Spain because the Dutch had been oppressed by Spain for many years. The Dutch aims in exploring the sea were political and economic. The Dutch were more interested in trade and commerce, which was less threatening to the Japanese. The Dutch did not have such a strong religious agenda for Japan because they were not backed by Rome.

Society and Culture during the Tokugawa Period

Tokugawa society was stratified into four main classes: samurai class (the military class), and the common population, which was divided into three classes—farmers, artisans, and merchants. Merchants and artisans mainly resided in cities, whereas farmers lived in rural areas.

The Tokugawa family ruled the nation with absolute force for 250 years. At the beginning of the Tokugawa period, there were 60,000 samurai. This number increased to 300,000 by the middle of the Tokugawa period. These samurai had various ranks, skills, and occupations. Samurai were professional soldiers who worked in the army and in the bureaucratic machine of the Tokugawa regime.

Strict Confucianism and samurai ethics together with Buddhism helped maintain this classification. Buddhism was made the national religion in order to eliminate Christianity. Everybody had to be a registered at a Buddhist temple or else they were killed. During this period, many Christians were martyred for their faith. Samurai ethics or the way of the warrior, *bushido*, affected many in society. *Bushido* emphasizes the ideal of selfless service to one's lord, which was manifested by ostentatious self-denial and the avoidance of drinking, gambling, extravagance, overeating, and visits to playhouses or brothels (Bowring and Kornicki, 1993). During the Tokugawa period, the emperor resided in Kyoto, whereas the Shogun resided in the capital city of Edo (contemporary Tokyo). The first Shogun, Ieyasu, chose Edo, which was then a small fishing community, to be his seat of government. He began to transform this town into a strong and suitable city. He started building programs, installed sewerage, and drained marshlands. He constructed a great fortress that was surrounded by a network of moats and he attracted merchants and craftsmen with offers of free land and tax concessions. Within a century, the Shogun's capital had developed into one of the largest cities in the world with over a million residents. Half of these belonged to the samurai class and the other half were people who provided services to the entire population—carpenters, porters, fishmongers, greengrocers, tea sellers, cake makers, pharmacists, fabric makers, etc. (Bowring and Kornicki, 1993).

In the 17th century, the emperor's capital, Kyoto, had a population of 600,000 people and Osaka was a commercial city that produced sake and oil. Japan became urbanized in the 17th century not due to an industrial revolution such as in Europe but rather due to the ambitious building and art projects of the Tokugawa shoguns starting with Ieyasu, the first Shogun. Some historical documents indicate that the government attempted to limit urbanization by encouraging immigrants to return to their rural areas.

The cities grew during this period and became increasingly rich due to merchants and commerce. This gave birth to a new group—merchant leaders. These leaders had economic power and included retailers, bankers, investors, and shipping and transportation magnates. Due to the rapid urbanization and the growth of commerce and arts, literacy was essential in Japan. In villages and cities all over Japan, children would go to learn to read and write at local temples. By the end of the Tokugawa period, schools had been established in some areas to teach literacy. The literacy rate in Japan was about 35%, which was higher than those of most other contemporary nations. This relatively high literacy rate gave rise to a printing industry and commercial printing of books and poems. There were commercial publishing companies that published various kinds of literature including stories, comic books, guide books, novels, religious literature, and pornography. The printing industry caused the Japanese to hunger for knowledge and this led to exploration in science and technology. The Dutch helped introduce Western medicine.

The Impersonalization of Japanese Citizens

All these political and social developments altered the social status of individuals; society crystallized into various vertical and horizontal groups based on bureaucratic levels. This process may be termed 'impersonalization.'

Confucianism played an important role in this process. Confucian thinking is based on the simple premise that there are natural distinctions within society based on status and occupation. This thinking emphasized absolute loyalty to one's superior. The Tokugawa regime used this principle to govern the nation. Another ideal of Confucianism was that no one should abuse his position. Rulers (including the government and administrators) should perform their duties as honestly as possible, regardless of their rank or status. However, this was just an ideal and was never perfectly realized in reality.

Based on these principles, Confucianism formed certain rules for fulfilling one's duty in a specific class or status. Every person belongs to a certain class or status and has his/her own specific duties. All duties begin with the family and the role within the family. The father has the highest status. Based on this, Confucianism assigned various duties and regulations between a man and his wife. Such duty-oriented regulations were generated for every institution or class ranging from the family to the government. During the Tokugawa period, the Japanese people were forced to live within the constraints of their social classes and to do what was required of them. The Tokugawa regime imposed these kinds of rules and regulations on the Japanese people for 250 years.

Bridge to Modernization

The Tokugawa period is considered to be a transitional period in Japan toward modernization and industrialization. Sydney Crawcour states that the roots of Japanese modernization are found in the Tokugawa period. He gives examples of the rapid developments that occurred in the final 50 years of the Tokugawa period including the modernization of the loan system and agricultural practices. Rural industries also grew rapidly. New commercial networks were formed and some industrial factories that were similar to those in the West were opened during the closing years of the Tokugawa period (Crawcour, 1974). At the end of this period, the population grew increasingly dissatisfied and many blamed the Shogun. In addition, Buddhist priests were the cause of dissatisfaction, corruption, and moral decay among the people and the population distrusted them and felt apathy toward Buddhism. Since the Emperor had no political role during this period, the Japanese people began to look to him since Shintoism, the Japanese traditional faith, venerates the Emperor. Consequently, Shintoism began to be revived.

Due to his unpopularity, the Shogun eventually resigned his power in 1867 and the Tokugawa period officially ended. In 1867, a new emperor came to power and ruled Japan until 1912. This period is called the Meiji period and it was a period of modernization.

Meiji Period (1868-1912)

The Meiji period began with an ambitious program aiming to transform Japan into a modern, centralized nation state in the West-European model—a nation that would be a strong military and economic power and that would be even better and more advanced than European states.

The Meiji period was characterized by the slogan *bunmei kaika* (which means civilization and enlightenment) and two other important slogans, *fukoku kyohei* (a rich nation with a strong army), and *oitsuki oikose* (catch and pass; i.e., catch up with and surpass the West). Intellectuals groups arose that viewed the West as offering civilization, science, and technology. One of these intellectuals was Fukuzawa Yukichi. He wrote several books on Western culture. Two of his important works are "An Outline of Civilization," and "Encouragement of Learning". Fukuzawa visited Western countries and described his observations of buildings, institutions, factories, streets, technology, etc. in his books. These things captured the imagination of the Japanese people. He believed that education was the foundation of modernity. Fukuzawa foundered one of the great universities of Japan — Keio University. However, while people like Fukuzawa accepted Western civilization, they strongly believed in maintaining Japanese culture and religion. Others had different opinions. They believed that the western model without Christianity and its values was empty and that Japan's modernization should progress in conjunction with accepting and adopting the Christian faith in Japan. Nakamura Masanao was one of these thinkers. However, others did not accept his ideas.

Soon a group of intellectuals formed to initiate reform in Japan. The central figures in the newly formed government came from various circles in society and they campaigned forcefully for the restoration of the Emperor's legitimate power and influence in national politics. These men were influenced by the writings and teachings of Fukuzawa and other scholars.

There were nine leaders, five of whom were from the samurai class. These leaders were called *genro*, which means "the elders". They all agreed that Japan was a weak, underdeveloped nation and that the only way for Japan to survive was to carefully develop her in the midst of aggressive imperialistic nations. The first thing they did was to implement a ground tax that was collected during the first 10 years of the Meiji period. It accounted for 80-90% of Japan's income.

The ground tax meant that peasants instead of paying a portion of the harvest as they did in the Tokugawa period now paid money for every piece of land they cultivated. Many poor peasants could not afford this new tax and so many went bankrupt or began to work for bigger landowners. This was the beginning of rural capitalism because peasants with small allotments could not survive and so they worked for peasants with larger farms instead. This also meant that peasants had to sell crops at markets to obtain money.

Japan began to change drastically. The law system changed. People were considered equal according to the new law and the old classes were no longer significant. However, this did not mean that Japanese people had totally abandoned the 250 year old class system. They continued practicing it since they could not instantly change to the new system. The political atmosphere changed in the 1870s when the first political parties were formed. In 1889, a constitution was effected that made provision for a bicameral parliament with an elected House of Representatives and an aristocratic House of Peers and a new legal system based on the French and German models (Hendry, 2004).

Foreign relations were improved and the isolationism of Japan began to end. This process had first commenced at the end of the Tokugawa period when the Tokugawa regime hired the Dutch, French, and the British to teach and train the army and teach foreign languages. This continued in the Meiji period. Foreigners were hired to help Japan with her modernization. The British assisted the Japanese in establishing railways, telegraph systems, and lighthouses. They also helped Japan modernize its navy. The French and Germans helped modernize the land forces (Bowring and Kornicki, 1993). However, the Japanese had made an important decision to catch up with the West and surpass western technology with the help of Japanese culture, especially Japanese Confucian ethics and Shinto and Buddhist teachings. This meant adopting western technology, science, education, and dress code. It also involved Japanese ethics and spirit such as the samurai emphasis on loyalty and honor. With this in mind, Meiji Japan began to industrialize. The goal was to be far superior and more advanced than the West.

Consequently, Japanese nationalism began to bloom. All the people had one goal in mind; namely, to transform Japan into a superpower. This is an interesting characteristic of Japan. History shows that Japan had imported many cultural, political, and technological concepts from China and Korea and now they were doing the same from the West. Japan has no problems making her own something that had originally been imported. I call this the 'Japanization process'— import something, impart it with a Japanese identity and improve it and even export it back to where the original idea had come from. This was also true after World War II in many different industries including cars and electronics. First, Japan learned to imitate and make cheap cars. Later an improved Japanese version of the cars was ready for export! Philips, a Dutch electronics company, invented the CD player. Japan took this concept and advanced the technology further than the Dutch did.

Industrialization

The industrialization of Japan was strongly motivated by the desire to make Japan a strong military power. Therefore, specific industries needed to be developed that could provide services, goods, and techniques to meet the modern military requirements of Japan. For example, iron needed to be manufactured for railways and for constructing western-style ships. This, in turn, necessitated the development of a mining industry. A communication industry was developed and telegraph lines were established to ease administrative control and communication between various administrations. The textile industry began to flourish. Western-style military uniforms were required since Japan wanted to modernize her army. Consequently, the cotton and woolen textile industries grew rapidly.

Despite this modernization and industrialization, there was an economic crisis between 1877 and 1880. High inflation devalued the land tax that the government depended on. Therefore, the government decided to privatize some non-strategic industries. However, it was difficult to find buyers for these industries so the government offered them at very low prices to people connected to the government and even to government officials. A few years later, the newly privatized industries became profitable and the few who had been privileged to purchase these enterprises grew wealthy and came to control a large share of Japan's modernized economy. This eventually resulted in much of Japanese industry being concentrated in a few giant corporations, known as the *zaibatsu* (Reischauer and Craig, 1989). Mitsui, Mitsubishi, Sumitomo, and Yasuda are important *zaibatsu* from this period.

Even today, *zaibatsu* have control over commerce and many industries, including banking, shipping, construction, and various other industries. Mitsubishi, for instance, is one of the *zaibatsu*. It not only manufactures machinery and vehicles, but it is also participates in banking and other services.

Political Ambitions during the Meiji Period

Japan's rising nationalism and political ambitions during this period caused problems with Japan's relationships with other Asian nations, especially China. As Japan grew stronger, friction between Japan and China increased with each seeking to dominate the Korean Peninsula. In 1882, they both stationed troops there (Bowring and Kornicki, 1993). This led to the Sino-Japanese War in 1894 and 1895. Japan won this war. In this war, Japan attacked Korea and then entered China through Korea. Shocked, the western nations had no choice but to recognize Japan as a strong Asian military power. Through a peace treaty, Japan received Taiwan as a territorial concession. This was the beginning of Japanese imperialistic ambitions. In 1905, Japan won another war, this time with Russia, a western nation. This also surprised the world. During the First World War, Japan allied with England and fought alongside the Allied Forces against Germany. Japan was viewed as an emerging world power at that point of history.

Religion

During the Meiji period, Confucian ethics together with Shinto and Buddhism, were merged and became the national religion of Japan. In contrast with the Tokugawa period, Christians were relatively free during the Meiji period. Christians played an important role in the formation of schools and universities. Christians also influenced the women's rights movement.

Japan During and After World War II

The attack on Pearl Harbor in 1941 marked the beginning of Japan's Pacific War against the Allied Forces, which ended with the unconditional surrender of Japan in 1945. The superpower ambitions and imperialist aspirations of Japan cost millions of lives in Asia and the Pacific. At the end, many Japanese people became victims themselves through the dropping of the atomic bombs on Hiroshima and Nagasaki. The Japan of 1945 was occupied, a conquered superpower and a fallen imperialist nation. All that remained were the ruins of war, chaos, poverty, and disease. Japan, in the summer of 1945, was a nation exhausted both physically and morally says the historian and writer, John W. Hall. According to Hall, since the outbreak of the war with China, 3.1 million Japanese (of whom 800,000 were civilians) had lost their lives.

Over 30% of Japanese lost their homes. There was a food shortage and the transportation system barely functioned. Acute food shortages brought much of the country to near starvation. Civilian morality broke down as farmers reaped tremendous profits by selling food on the black market. Wealthy families bartered heirlooms for the necessities of life. The industry had been smashed to one quarter of its previous capacity and the country was on the verge of inflation. The people were also emotionally and intellectually bewildered having been feed exaggerated wartime propaganda and hyper-nationalist values, all of which collapsed with Japan's unconditional surrender (Hall, 1991). Japan fell under the supervision of the Supreme Commander of Allied Powers (SCAP) under the leadership of General Douglas MacArthur. According to the SCAP's policy, Japan had to go through three important phases: demilitarization, democratization, and rehabilitation.

Japan was totally dismantled. Certain laws that had been imposed in the Meiji period were rescinded. Also, acknowledgement of the deity of the Japanese emperor was abolished. Democratic laws were imposed and political parties played an important role in the political scene. Japan was economically revived. The Korean War in the 1950s provided an economic boost to Japan since Japan supplied US forces in Korea with various goods and services.

Life slowly began to return to normal and the Japanese people regained their self-confidence. In the early 1950s and 1960s, new technologies revived some industries that had been damaged during the war such as the shipbuilding industry. Later, electronic devices such as radios entered the international economic scene. The automobile industry began to flourish. Later, the computer industry began to bloom. Society began to change. Western lifestyles with some basic Japanese values were increasingly adopted. These values were adopted by the management of Japanese companies and businessmen, which the Japanese call *salary man*, who represent the working class in the private and public sectors, began to be an important group in Japanese society. For many years, Japan had a low unemployment and crime rates, although they have been increasing recently.

Once again, Japan became a world superpower. However, Japanese society is beginning to change. Unhappy youth and a monotonous modern society are generating new social problems. Suicide and other social problems are increasing in Japan. The Japanese game industry and the Internet have resulted in many living isolated lives, especially the youth. Japan has become a pioneer in pornographic movies and magazines and an exporter of such videos and DVDs to other nations. Pornographic sites combined with advanced Internet and computer technology have reduced the moral values of Japanese society. These are some side effects of an overdose of 'modernity.'

JAPANESE

SOCIETY

PART **TWO**

Chapter Three

Japanese Family

To understand the Japanese family and even Japanese society it is essential to know about the traditional Japanese family system, which is called *ie*. According to Reischauer and Graig, the pre-modern Japanese family or *ie* might include a subordinate branch of a family, which was under the authority of the main family, and other members who were distant relatives or were not related at all. The father or family council had absolute authority over individual members. This kind of family existed particularly among the more prominent members of the feudal warrior class, rich merchants, and certain peasant groups (Reischauer and Graig, 1989). *Ie* is the indigenous term for family; however, it does not convey the exact meaning of the word 'family' as we use it in the West. *Ie* can be translated as 'house' or 'building,' but it is also used in a broader sense as 'family' or 'kin.' It included a whole structure that consisted of the main family under which were various subfamilies.

In her book, *Understanding Japanese Society*, Joy Hendry writes that continuity is a very important feature of the *ie*. The individual members of a particular house, who need not always be resident, represent the living members of that particular *ie*. The total membership includes those of all generations: ancestors who had been forgotten as individuals, those who had died more recently and who were still remembered, and descendants who have not yet been born (Hendry, 2004). Traditional Japanese houses contain a Buddhist altar known as a *butsudan* at which family members venerate their ancestors (*senzo*) and recently deceased individuals of the ie. *Butsudan* played an important role in the house. When family members made important decisions or discussed important matters they opened the door of the butsudan so that the ancestors may listen and participate in the family discussion.

Ie was a hierarchical family system based on the Confucian principles of honor and loyalty, which applied to all relationships in the *ie*. Old–young relationships were based on loyalty and indebtedness and relationships were duty oriented. Duty toward the members in the *ie* system was considered more important than anything else. This duty-based system affected the relationship between men and women: men had a much higher status than women. Women were required to provide for their husband's every need. Consequently, in the *ie* system, marriages were arranged based on social status and the suitability of the women to fulfill her duty to the *ie* of her husband. Love between husband and wife was not considered essential and a lack of love was not considered to hinder the duty of a couple to each other and to the *ie* system.

After the surrender of Japan and the victory of the Allied forces in 1945, the new government abolished the *ie* family system. In the new constitution, the family was defined as a nuclear unit rather than a collection of various family units and women were treated equally with men so that they enjoyed the same rights as men. However, the abolition of the *ie* system does not mean that it is completely dismissed by today's society. Japan practiced this family system for centuries. Although the *ie* system does not exist legally, it still affects various aspects of society. For example, I believe that the *zaibastu* business culture is strongly based on the *ie* system. Some aspects of relationships are still influenced by the *ie* system. For example, even though women are legally equal with men in some aspects, they are still treated inferior to men.

The Contemporary Japanese Family

Views on the Japanese traditional family system are gradually changing. The contemporary Japanese family resembles the traditional Western family with father, mother, and children living in little apartments in urban areas. The mother cares for the children while the father works in a company or government institution or runs his own business.

How does a typical modern Japanese family function? It all begins at home. Japanese people have a very particular concept of home known as *uchi*, which literary means 'home' but also means 'inside.' Everything outside the home is referred to as *soto*, which literary means 'outside.' However, *uchi–soto* does not just refer to the literal home or to inside and outside; rather, it is a form of the *ie* family system. In this case, *uchi* means home and everything internal. It may also be related to clean, beautiful, and everything associated with good. *Uchi* may also be related to the *ie* to which someone belongs. Conversely, *soto* refers to outside and external territories, but it can also be related to dirty, unclean, etc. That is why Japanese people remove their shoes when they enter their homes (*uchi*) so that they will not bring dirt from outside (*soto*) into their homes. Chapter eleven discusses the *uchi–soto* system within a cultural framework.

Children

We commence our analysis of the Japanese family with the children. From an early age, children are trained to be aware of hierarchy and to find their place at home and outside. Children are trained to think and act in the group they belong to and then to act individually. From a very early age, they are trained to consider the good of others and to do to others as they would want others to do to them. Japanese kids are raised to be group oriented rather than self-oriented. Consequently, they may belong to different groups in different contexts. They have to act for the sake and harmony of the uchi to which they belong, which may consist of their siblings at home, their friends at kindergarten, or their classmates at school.

The personal collective term mina-san is used to address and refer to the whole group and its needs. Any individual whose behavior is detrimental to mina-san is made to feel most uncomfortable (Hendry, 2004). There is a saying in Japanese, *deru kugi wa utareru*, which means "the protruding nail will be hammered down." This proverb is a very good example of the manner in which children are trained from an early age. Also, they are trained at school not to talk much and not to ask many questions because it may disturb the group and thus may be considered selfish.

In nuclear families, it was common for the wife to stay at home, raise the children, and be involved in the matters of the house, uchi. This is gradually changing in contemporary Japan. Most married women now work. Parents are too busy to look after their children. Consequently, the number of children is decreasing. In early postwar Japan, husbands worked and wives took care of their children. This state of affairs is becoming increasingly unusual and children receive little love from their parents. Children spend a lot of time alone. The introduction of computers and the Internet have worsened this situation. Children communicate by the Internet and mobile phones while contact with the outside world is diminishing. As a result, many of them have mental problems or will develop them in the future.

In 2002, BBC World News reported the following: "Teenage boys in Japan's cities are turning into modern hermits—never leaving their rooms: hikikomori! Pressure from schools and an inability to talk to their families are suggested causes."[1]

Hikikomori are adolescents and young adults who feel overwhelmed by Japanese society. They feel unable to fulfill their expected roles in society and react by withdrawing from society. Hikikomori often refuse to leave their parents' homes and may lock themselves in a single room for months or even years. According to some estimates, there may be one million hikikomori in Japan or one out of 10 young men. Most of them are male and many of them are the eldest sons.

There is a lot of pressure on adolescents and young adults in Japan. The people around them expect them to be 'successful.' This pressure comes from several different sources. One of the biggest concerns for Japanese adolescents is their performance in the educational system where they often experience significant pressure from parents and society in general. In extreme cases, this pressure starts before they enter preschool when they have to pass an entrance exam to get into the best preschool. Preschool prepares children for the entrance exam

---

1- http://news.bbc.co.uk/2/hi/programmes/correspondent/2334893.stm

to enter the best kindergarten, which in turn prepares children for the entrance exam to the best primary school, junior high school, high school, and eventually university. Another source of pressure is other students who may harass or bully some students for various reasons including obesity, ethnicity, or a perceived lack of intelligence, sporting ability, or money. Some students have been punished for bullying and truancy that brings shame to their families.

Women, Wives & Mothers

Marriage and Housewives

Traditionally, housewives have been praised as the selfless, hardworking, and devoted mothers who helped bring about the country's economic miracle. They made sure that their children were educated and that their husbands stayed focused on their careers. There was a clear division of labor between men and women, with the role of women being to nurture and strengthen children and men. (Hirata and Warschauer, 2014). Many people still expect women to fulfill this role. Japanese companies are generally not open toward women who try to balance career and family life. Thus, 70% of working women quite their jobs when they have their first child, and some take part-time jobs once their children are at school or grown up. These women quit their jobs in their late twenties or their thirties, and then rejoin the labor force once their child is older, with a peak in participation from age 45 to 49 (ibid). Housework is considered to be the domain of the Japanese wife. A housekeeper is too expensive for most families, and with salarymen husbands working late evenings, wives are the only ones left to clean up. Mothers spend most of their time on childcare, cooking, and cleaning (ibid).

Most marriages in Japan are arranged *(miai)*. Usually women marry as the result of introductions made by others. However, young people think such traditional matchmaking is old-fashioned, and only about 5% of current marriages are made possible through traditional match making. According to Hirata and Warschauer, single people who can afford it instead turn to professional marriage brokers, stimulating a booming industry in post-3/11 Japan, as young people, aware of their mortality after the tragedy, seek *kizuna* ('bonding'). Men and women pay a fee to the marriage broker, and provide information about themselves and their preferred partners, including income, height, and educational background (Hirata and Warschauer, 2014).

It is difficult to judge how many marriages are based on affection. Most contemporary couples describe their marriages as 'in between', which means that someone introduced them and they subsequently fell in love and decided to marry. Love alone is not viewed as a sufficiently solid basis for marriage. The young Japanese couple is more cognizant than its American counterpart of the need for social support to keep a marriage going. Family investigations are an important precursor for marriage decisions and a Japanese man or woman is still unlikely to marry someone who their family opposes (Imamura, 1990).

Working Mothers

Although the position of women in Japanese society is changing rapidly, women are still discriminated against in the workplace. Most women earn less than their male counterparts and it is quite difficult for women to get high positions in a company or organization. Women account for only 0.1% of board member positions in Japan's top companies. On the other hand, Japan's economic difficulties are pushing mothers into the workplace. Many Japanese men today want their wives to work full time to help meet family expenses. According to Hirata and Warschauer, having a career and a family might seem as though it would make a woman's life more financially secure and emotionally satisfying, but that is not necessarily the case. Hirata and Warschauer report that working women in Japan remain burdened with a disproportionately unbalanced share of the housework and childcare, making the life of the working mom even harder than it is (Hirata and Warschauer, 2014).

The duties of the wife do not just consist of caring for her household, husband, and children. The fact that Japanese people (especially women) have the highest life expectancy in the world makes life harder for wives because they have to care for elderly family members who live longer and thus require special care and attention. These responsibilities make it difficult for wives to hold a full-time job. Due to insufficient aid for working parents and not enough daycare centers and preschools, and since family life is not expected to interfere with the husband's work, mothers choose to leave their jobs for the sake of educating and raising their children. This is a major burden on the wife. Many women have recently been delaying marriage and children in favor of their careers. Many women do not want to marry and remain single, whereas others get married but chose not to have children. This produces other social problems; for example, the average age for getting married is increasing and there is a record number of single-parent households and childless households.

Single Women

Hirata and Warschauer suggest that the traditional idea that all women will be office ladies until they become housewives is no longer true. They categorize the adult women into three cultures: single women, housewives, and working mothers. Each category reflects its own unique worldviews and challenges that surpass simply economic status (ibid). Single women are often worried about financial security. The statistics present a terrifying glimpse of their future: among single women aged 20–63, nearly a third live below the poverty line. This means that 31.6% of single women earn less than 1.25 million yen ($12,500) per year. For those over 64, the rate is even worse, at 52% (ibid).

Men, Husbands and Fathers

Post-war Japanese families are often referred to as 'fatherless' families. Here, the term 'fatherless' describes two common situations: families where the father has little time to be with his family due to long working days and families where the father is absent due to divorce or separation. Both situations are alarmingly common in Japan.

Japanese fathers are not very involved with their children. Long working hours and after work drinks with colleagues mean that fathers are away from home most of the day. Consequently, they have little time to spend with their wives and children. On average, fathers spend 17 minutes a day with their children and helping looking after them (Masako Ishii-Kuntz, 2004). Japanese fathers are often viewed as borderline absentee fathers. They are described with the well-known proverb 'a good husband is healthy and absent.' Many wives want the salary, but not so many want the man (Hirata and Warschauer, 2014).

The second case, the real 'fatherless' families where there is no father at home at all, is increasing daily. A Japanese government survey published in early 2005 estimated that the number of genuinely fatherless families has increased dramatically to 1.22 million families in fiscal year 2003. This is the highest number of fatherless families ever registered in the history of Japan. It indicates a 28.3% increase from the previous survey conducted in 2000. The figures also reveal that the vast majority of children in these households live far below the poverty line, creating a rapidly expanding underclass of impoverished families. In February 2005, a 27 year old woman and her three year old son were found starved to death in their apartment in Saitama prefecture near Tokyo. Police reported that there was no food in the apartment and the woman only had eight yen (0.07 US dollars) in her purse (J. Sean Curtin, 2005).

The 28.3% increase in fatherless families is due to the growing divorce rate in Japan, which is, in turn, due to changing lifestyles. Fathers who are too busy to fulfill their responsibilities as husbands and fathers are the key cause for the dissolution of a strong family fellowship. The lack of a strong paternal influence and responsibility in homes has many negative effects on society. It is apparent that workaholic fathers create 'fatherless' homes, which have generated a rash of teenage angst and occasionally shocking outbursts of violence.

A report by an advisory panel to the Education Minister states that "fathers who do not understand what it means to raise children and who do not cooperate in the process are causing anxiety among many children and mothers." As fathers are increasingly absent at home, children tend to read their mother's faces and try to be a 'good' boy or girl to please their mothers. Children tend to view their fathers more as a friend than as a parent and they do not receive enough discipline from them regarding what is good and bad.

Herbivores – Soshoku-kei danshi

The Japanese men are also changing. In 2006, Maki Fukasawa coined the term 'herbivore men', or in Japanese *soshoku-kei danshi*, to describe the 20 to 30-year-olds of the post-bubble generation (Hirata and Warschauer, 2014). The herbivores are characterized by their passivity and are compared to grass-eaters, content to graze on whatever grows naturally around them, rather than aggressively pursuing their ambitions and desires. Unlike the salarymen, herbivores are described as 'metrosexuals' meaning they are especially careful about their appearance and typically spend a significant amount time on shopping and grooming. However, having grown up in the post-bubble era, herbivores are skeptical of expensive purchases. They might carry around 'points cards' to save money at stores (ibid).

As a reaction to the culture of the bubble economy, herbivores are not interested in devoting their lives to a company at the expense of their inner life. It seems that they lack ambition; they work, but they maintain a spiritual independence. They see their jobs as a source of emotional satisfaction and a way to get by. Their identity is not linked to a company, but to a particular hobby. They reject most corporate norms and are more likely invest in hobbies than in performance goals for their company. While herbivores do not have strong career ambitions, they are careful not to loose it either. They avoid risk in their careers and personal lives, and they often do only the bare minimum required to get by. While not indebted to their companies, many herbivores would be happy to hold one job for their entire working life (ibid).

The herbivore phenomenon hinges on Japan's changing society and economy. In the post-bubble era, families have produced fewer children and schools have fewer students. In a less competitive environment, young people have grown up more comfortable with themselves. They have received the attention they craved, and are more secure. They do not seek validation in competition with their school peers, and this attitude is carried through into their adult lives. A consulting company to Japan's largest advertising firm estimates that the proportion of Japanese young men who consider themselves herbivores ranges from 60% of men in their early twenties to at least 42% of men aged 23–34 (ibid).

Otaku men

In addition to salarymen and herbivores, there are the Otaku men. In the 1990s, the word otaku was used for people who spent much of their free time at home. The word literally means 'your home' – the 'o' indicating politeness. The otaku are described as socially incompetent, but often excellent technological shut-ins (ibid). Currently, the Otaku men are generally referred to as geeks or nerds who are extremely passionate about their hobbies, including anime, games, trains, military equipment, idols in the entertainment industry, and much more (ibid).

Fertility & No Urge for Sex

A 2010 survey conducted by the National Institute of Population and Social Security Research shows that 61.4% of never-married men between 18–34 years old had no girlfriend. This is, again, much higher compared to data from 2005, when this same statistic was 52.2% , with 27.6% of men in that age range reporting that they were not even looking for a mate. Further, the Japan Family Planning Association reports that, in 2010, 36.1% of males indicated being indifferent to having sex. This is a huge increase compared to 17.5% in 2008. As for those in their late thirties, more than 25% of unmarried men and women between 35-39 years old say they have never had sex. Though the significance of these findings has been questioned, comparisons to previous surveys by the same organizations point to a downward trend in male–female relationships among young people in Japan."[2]

Due to economic pressures, married couples are also sharing less physical intimacy. A 2010 survey suggests that the number of married couple having no sex in the previous months has increased from 31.0% in 2004 to 40.8%, with many stating that work-related fatigue was an important factor (Hirata and Warschauer, 2014). Such behavior may be one of the factors of the low birthrate in Japan. According to a 2010 survey by the National Institute of Population and Social Security Research, 60.4% of women cited cost as the reason they had fewer children than they wanted. [3]

Divorce in Japan

The divorce rate has increased by 48% since the 1990s. Currently, more than 20% of Japanese marriages are dissolved by divorce. There are various reasons for this increase. The prolonged economic recession is one reason, especially among couples with low educational backgrounds. These low-income households are vulnerable to salary cuts and an unexpected job loss leads to accumulating debts and even foreclosure. When the husband is not able to provide the daily necessities (as he is traditionally expected to do) and the family debt becomes overwhelming, most women decide to live on their own and start their lives all over again.

Forced marriages or shotgun weddings, known as *dekichatta kekkon* in Japanese, are another reason for the growing divorce rate in Japan. A shotgun wedding is a form of forced marriage in response to an unexpected pregnancy. In traditionally conservative societies such as Japan, both the woman and the man will lose face in their community and therefore the man involved is obligated to marry the woman before her pregnancy becomes noticeable. It is estimated that 25% of all marriages in Japan are based on *dekichatta kekkon.*

---

2 - National Institute of Population and Social Security, 2011: http://www.ipss.go.jp/site-ad/index_english/nfs14/Nfs14_Couples_Eng.pdf
3 - Ibid.

Another interesting phenomenon is the growing divorce rate among middle-aged and aged couples between 45 and 64 years old, which quadrupled between 1960 and 2005. When men retire, they start spending a lot of time at home. They feel empty because they have been devoted to their work for their entire working lives. Housewives have their own social networks and so do not feel lonely, which enhances the sense of alienation that husbands feel at home. This causes tension between wives and husbands, as their mismatched emotional states lead to disagreements. Furthermore, areas of disagreement that were latent while the couple spent most of their days apart now rise to the surface. This increases the stress and pressure on housewives, which often leads to various illnesses such as ulcers and skin rashes. Some older wives, after many years of fulfilling their marriage duties, decide to get divorced. In 2007, due to legislation passed in 2003, women who filed for divorce were entitled to half their husbands' pensions. This has encouraged more women to file for divorce.

Lastly, due to the influence of the media, divorce has gradually become to be considered less of a taboo topic. Of course, it is still a difficult topic to discuss in Japanese society; yet it is gradually becoming more acceptable, especially in large cities where there is considerably less social pressure than in small towns or rural areas. Just like any other society, divorce in Japan has adversely affected many children and families. However, Japan faces an additional challenge due to the increasing divorce rate: the relatively underdeveloped social welfare system. In the past, Japan's social welfare system has relied strongly on families to provide care, assistance, and resources to family members in need. The increasing divorce rate is shaking the foundations of such a family-based social welfare system. The aging society requires more care and services, but the government is not prepared for the steadily increasing demand for care and social welfare. The Japanese government faces immense challenges as it struggles to offer adequate services to its rapidly aging population.

The Elderly

It is appropriate to end this chapter with a discussion of the elderly, as this age group will have the last word on Japan's future. Japanese society is getting older. The birth rate is decreasing. It is estimated that in 2040, one third of the population will be over 65 years old and only 11% will be under 14 (Hendry, 2004).

In 2009, only 13% of Japan's population is under 15 years old. According to Jeff Kingston, the low fertility rate is due to women finding it difficult to juggle work and family responsibilities. Kingston writes:

"As a result, many working women are delaying or forgoing marriage altogether, while a growing number of those who marry choose not to have children. As attitudes and social norms have changed, and lifestyles diversify, getting married and having children is no longer the default option it once was. Women who are now enjoying greater social and economic freedom wonder if having kids is really what they want, and consider carefully what they stand to lose by raising a family, especially given that their husbands (and their employers) continue to shift most of the child-rearing burden on them"(Kingston, 2010).

The combination of the low fertility rate and long life expectancy (the life expectancy in 2009 was 86.05 years for women and 79.29 years for men) makes Japan a very aged society. This long life expectancy is a consequence of a healthy food culture among the middle aged and elderly. However, as a result of increasing globalization, consumption of fast food is increasing, along with other unhealthy eating habits, smoking tobacco, and alcohol consumption. These trends threaten to cause serious long-term problems for Japan's healthcare system. Even though the Japanese government has implemented various reforms for elderly care (especially since 2000), Japan's current healthcare infrastructure is unable to cope with the growing number of elderly people. There will be fewer young people available to care for the elderly.

Japan's healthcare system faces serious shortages of doctors, nurses, and caregivers, especially in rural areas. There are currently 270,000 doctors in Japan, which is equivalent to about two doctors per 1,000 people. This is the lowest doctor–patient ratio in G8 countries and the third lowest in the 34-member OECD. To reach the average doctor–patient ratio for OECD countries, Japan requires 140,000 more doctors, an increase of about 50% (Kingston, 2010). This could be a focus of future Christian missionary endeavors, combining evangelism with medical services. On a non-governmental level, caring for the elderly is already problematic in Japan. A growing number of elderly people are unable and unwilling to rely on family members to help them through the final years of their lives (Hendry, 2004).

According to Hirata and Warschauer, there are two contradictory problems related to seniors in Japan: "the elderly in Japan are simultaneously too powerful and too poor" (Hirata and Warschauer, 2014). The voting participation among elderly is very high and, because of that, seniors exercise greater political influence than in any other country in the world. They influence legislation and political decisions often that advantage them rather than the younger population. The impact of the elderly on the workforce is also quite negative (ibid).

The hierarchical culture in Japanese companies gives seniors more power and influence, leaving fewer opportunities for the younger generation. Thus, a person's age, rather than by the quality of that person's work or ideas, is largely responsible for the pay and power afforded to individuals in Japanese companies. Hirata and Warschauer give an example of one study that examined the backgrounds of 150 CEOs from the top 50 enterprises in Korea, China, and Japan: The CEOs in Japan were the oldest, with an average age of 63.1, compared to only 51 in China. The Japanese CEOs also had the least education: only 18% had graduate degrees, compared to about 50% of the Korean CEOs and fully 70% of the Chinese. These discrepancies were attributed to Japan's 'unique corporate culture,' where 'experience is valued' (ibid).

On the other hand, the power of seniors in Japan has not led to their prosperity. The lower ratio of working-age population to elderly means fewer resources available to support seniors with healthcare and welfare. The problem is even worsened further by the fact that a smaller percentage of working-age women hold jobs than in most other developed countries (ibid). Therefore, government has been cutting benefits for seniors by shifting the burden of care to the elderly themselves. For instance, according to the law, upper-middle-income seniors aged 70 and above have to cover 30% of their own medical bills. Though many Japanese seniors enjoy relatively good corporate pensions, others receive more meager state pensions or no pension at all (ibid).

Lonely Elders

Despite the romantic image of the elderly spending time with their families and grandchildren, many of them are actually spending their closing years isolated from the younger generation. One indication of the yearning for an ideal family complete with grandchildren is revealed by the demand for a paid service called 'service of the heart.' One company, which has provided such a 'rent-a-family' service since 1990, reported that the demand for this service is so high that they have had to place many elderly couples and individuals on a waiting list for visits from hired 'family members'. A typical rent-a-family session simulates a three-generation family setting. The 'daughter' or 'daughter-in-law'—a trained entertainer—prepares meals at which all eat together. There are other 'family' events such as family walks in the park, exchanging gifts, singing, chatting, and playing with 'grandchildren' who usually climb on the 'grandparents' laps and play games with them (Thang, 2002). This sad but true anecdote indicates that Japanese society, especially the family, is not improving but rather is heading in the wrong direction. This is caused by the lack of interaction between members of families, on which society is based. It is important to mention that abuse of the elderly is increasing in contemporary Japan. Most of this abuse comes from overburdened family members and caregivers in the form of psychological abuse, negligence or denial of care, and economic abuse, which involves selling possessions that the elderly person does not want sold. However, many of the abusers are reportedly unaware of the negative consequences of their behavior and do not consider that what they are doing constitutes abuse.

Elderly Crimes

In 2012, about 540,000 seniors were living alone on state welfare. Poverty and desperation sometimes drive seniors to crime, and criminality among older people is rising rapidly in Japan, where it used to be virtually unknown. Meanwhile, the general crime rate has been falling by about 5% a year. Elderly crime has been growing much faster than the national crime rate. The number of seniors in the country who were the subject of criminal investigation went up to 16%, a six-fold increase from 2001 to 2011, and the number of assaults committed by seniors increased nearly fifty-fold in the same decade. Hirata and Warschauer speak of 'seniorization' of Japanese prisons:

Most imprisoned seniors commit their first crime after the age of 65. Three-quarters of senior prisoners are repeat offenders: they mostly commit serial petty crimes, such as shoplifting for food or picking pockets, to cope with cuts in government welfare spending and rising healthcare costs. A quarter of senior offenders have been arrested ten times or more and have returned to prison within a year of each release. By international standards, Japan has an unusually high rate of offenders aged 60 and above – about 12%, compared to a typical rate of 5% in other advanced industrialized countries" (Hirata and Warschauer, 2014).

Chapter Four

Japanese Working Life

The Japanese are known as hard-working people. They work long hours and are almost never absent from work. This is the image many have of the Japanese working force. This chapter considers Japanese working life and culture and their impact on society. A Japanese employee is generally referred to as *salary man*, an English loan word that has entered Japanese.

It is important to realize that Japan is a group-oriented society. This means a huge emphasis is placed on the group and belonging to the group. As mentioned above, the Japanese refer to such groups as *uchi*, which means both 'house' and 'inside' and generally refers to the family. However, *uchi* does not refer just to the family; it can have various other meanings depending on the context. In this case, the company or the place where people work becomes *uchi* and the colleagues become family members.

Japanese companies function quite differently from their European and American counterparts. However, this has changed in recent years. Japan basically has a lifetime employment system. This means the workers generally work in the same company for their entire working lives. A unique Japanese company culture and lifestyle has developed from this principle. Schools and universities often have contracts with companies so that immediately after their students graduate some of them enter these companies. For decades, this was how many were recruited and it was one of the reasons why Japan had a low unemployment rate. This is why group activities, group performance of various services, and company benefits are important in Japan. Working in Japan requires not just doing your job skillfully but also fitting in with the company culture. The Japanese feel it is important to love their company.

In Japan, it has been believed that the morals and mental attitudes of the individual have an important bearing on productivity. Loyalty to the company has been highly regarded. A man may be an excellent technician, but if his way of thinking and morals differ from those of the company, the company will not hesitate to dismiss him. Men who enter a company after working for another company at a comparatively advanced stage in their working lives tend to be difficult to mold and their loyalties are suspect (Nakane, 1970). Since this lifetime employment system is a family-like group, it pervades the private lives of the employees. This is crucial for group unity because the individual's total emotional participation in a group helps form a closed world and results in group independence or isolation (ibid).

Companies provide various services and benefits to their employees such as pensions, health care, and often accommodation (e.g., dormitories for unmarried workers, apartments for families, and even large houses for senior employees). They also sometimes provide sports facilities and holiday resorts for employees. In some companies, sexual activities for male employees are common. Some companies believe that sexual intercourse relieves stress. Some companies that lack the resources to hire prostitutes provide special rooms where employees may watch pornographic movies to release their stress.

In return, employees are expected to perform to the very best of their abilities. They are also expected to take few holidays and spend their leisure time with their colleagues drinking in local bars, playing sport together, or going on office trips.

Within the group-oriented system, there are peer level and junior/senior interactions on individual levels. In most companies, the president is considered the father of the house. As such, he may intervene in the private lives of his employees such as finding a spouse for an employee or acting as a matchmaker. Another aspect of Japanese working life concerns the company you belong to. Japanese people do not ask what you do for a living; rather, they want to know which company you work for. Working in Japan means belonging to a group that is your working family, especially for big companies or institutions. Each institution may have its own song or anthem;

singing this song promotes a sense of unity among employees and employers.

Most big companies also conduct various religious rituals. For example, a very famous electronic company has a special sanctuary for worshiping gods and ancestors who became gods. There are also statutes of famous Japanese and international scientists such as Thomas Edison (who is honored as the god of electricity) for employees to venerate. These kinds of rituals are rooted in Japanese culture and are still practiced in many major companies.

During my research, I discovered that some Japanese companies have created a sort of their own company "religion" with rites and ceremonies designed to bolster the work atmosphere and sense of unity. Most Japanese companies do not want to employ people who are members of religious organizations because they feel that their loyalties will be divided. Thomas P. Rohlen conducted a case study of a Japanese bank and studied its management and working culture. In his book, *For Harmony and Strength*, he describes the ceremonies that were conducted. He discusses the various catechisms recited during the entrance ceremony when joining the company. Company employees sing the company anthem together. He found out that the bank does not want to employ members of 'new religions' that demand considerable time and effort from their members. This is not because the bank considers these religions inherently bad; on the contrary, the bank views many of them as being positive moral forces. But the bank does not want its employees to have divided loyalties. Furthermore, the religious behavior of the parents of a potential employee is important: the bank is not interested in employing the children of religious zealots (Rohlen, 1974).

As it is mentioned above, Japanese companies have created their own religion and what they practice is no less a religion than that practiced by religious organizations. The practice of not employing people who are members of a religious organization indicates the competition that exists between the 'company religion' and conventional religions.

Lifetime employment is changing

The lifetime employment system described above is changing very rapidly along with work ethics and values. An EPA survey conducted in 1999 revealed that the number of companies offering lifetime employment fell from 27.1% in 1990 to only 9.9% in 1999, while companies abandoning lifetime employment increased from 36.4 to 45.3% in that same period. The percentage of companies in limbo between lifetime employment and some other personnel policy increased from 25.4 to 38.3% (Matsumoto, 2002). Matsumoto writes:

> *As Japanese companies increasingly abandon lifetime employment, many are adopting a merit system in their labor management practices (reported in the EPA survey report of 1999). This type of system rewards abilities and achievements and no doubt reflects the demands of increased world competition on Japanese businesses and the changing attitudes of the contemporary Japanese worker. These changes in Japanese companies have been accompanied by changes in the attitudes of Japanese employees (ibid).*

Related to the changes in lifetime employment, Matsumoto notes a change in the degree of loyalty of contemporary salarymen. These men used to be viewed as "samurai in suits" who were the backbone of the Japanese economy (ibid). Usually a man looks for a company to spend his life working there, financially supporting the family and getting personal satisfaction from the company work, while his wife cares for the household and children, regardless of whether she works or not. According to Hirata and Warschauer, salarymen have image problems and are losing respect. In the days when the economy was booming, the salarymen were viewed as an earnest, selfless, hard-working segment of society, contributing to Japan's economic growth. Yet today, the image of the salarymen is changing; they are considered to be clumsy and unattractive people. Recently in the media, the salaryman has been portrayed a trapped, spineless slave of his company, who endures insults like *shachiku* ('corporate livestock') or *kaisha no inu* ('corporate dog') (Hirata and Warschauer, 2013).

According to *The Economist*, what used to be the cornerstone of the economy, namely the paternalistic relationship between Japan's companies and their employees, is crumbling. Due to a large generational shift, today's young professionals refuse to make work the center of their lives or to accept the hardships and corporate paternalism of earlier decades. These labor-market forces manifest themselves in several ways. They affect gender equality, as more women enter the workforce. They touch on immigration, as foreigners are recruited to do jobs that Japanese do not want to do. They are changing the role of older people, as many pensioners re-enter the workforce. They also have distributional consequences. Japan is one of the most egalitarian of the world's rich societies, yet it now has one of the highest proportions of "working poor"—people who have jobs but can barely make ends meet. Wages have fallen by around 10% (in nominal terms) over the past decade.[1]

Performance-Based System

Japan does not just have major enterprises and institutions. Most companies are medium or small enterprises such as family businesses. These companies differ from large companies. Of course, loyalty to the company and the group is still important for medium and small companies. However, these companies are unable to provide the same benefits as large companies. This does not mean that loyalty is not strong in these companies. On the contrary, because of their smaller size, group unity is more important than for larger companies.

Japanese society is changing rapidly and this affects working life in Japan. In contemporary Japan, there is a growing shift from a lifetime employment system to a performance-based system. Performance-based systems no longer pay employees based on their seniority and length of time at a company, but rather based on their performance and achievements.

---

1 - "Employment in Japan: Sayonara, Salaryman" , The Economist, January 3, 2008, accessed December 22, 2014, http://www.economist.com/node/10424391 .

Fruiitaa

Another tendency in Japanese working culture is for young people to work part time and have more than one job. Such people are called *furiitaa*, which means 'free person' since they are free from the constraints imposed by the lifestyle of a typical salaryman. According to Matsumoto: "the stereotype of the Japanese salaryman who is willing to sacrifice himself and his family, who is happy to be a worker bee for the sake of company and country, and who does not relish rewards based on individual achievements is more myth than reality, especially among younger workers" (Matsumoto, 2002).

Neither the Japanese lifetime employment system nor a performance-based system is healthy for society. The former may provide economic stability and a low unemployment rate, but its working culture and group expectations adversely affect family life. Fathers are often fatigued and have little time to spend with their families. Even in the UK and US, siblings meet much more frequently than typical Japanese. Christmas is an occasion when relatives gather together. New Year's Day is the Japanese equivalent to Christmas. Everyone is busy with preparations for visits from subordinate staff and they then in turn visit their superiors. People have little time or energy to visit collateral kin such as married brothers, sisters, cousins, uncles, and aunts, although parents and grandparents will certainly be visited if they do not live in the same house (Nakane, 1970). They are bound to be negative repercussions for society when work becomes more important than family. People will soon become fatigued, frustrated, and hurting.

The *furiitaa* phenomenon is a reaction to both systems since *furiitaa* have opted out of both systems. *Furiitaa* want to be free. However, too much freedom may give rise to another social phenomenon known as 'parasite singles.' These are singles between the ages of 20 and 35 who remain dependent on their parents. While they live with them, they do not pay rent nor do housework. They have various part-time jobs and spend their money on expensive clothing and jewelry. They sometimes go on shopping trips to neighboring countries such as Korea.

Chapter Five

Social Stratification in Japan

If you visit Japan for business, you will notice that when two people meet for the first time they immediately exchange business cards. This is a very important custom in Japan because it informs the other person of your status so that they will know where they stand relative to you. The information on the business card will affect the mannerisms and treatment used. Even the language used will be based on the relative positions of the two people. The lower rank person will bow deeper than the other person.

How do the Japanese conceptualize social stratification? The Japanese equivalents of the words class and stratum, *kaikyu* and *kaiso*, are both terms translated from English. The Japanese have a clear conception of stratification in their society even if their notions may be conceptually identical to their Western counterparts. Several Japanese terms describe social stratification. *Kaku* denotes a finite series of ranks. It is a generic term that can be applied to a wide range of ranking systems. *Mibun* implies the status into which a person is born. The term *kakei*, family line, has a similar connotation, but it emphasizes lineage and pedigree more. In contrast, *chii* refers to status a person achieves over time (Sugimoto, 2002).

In her book, *Japanese Society*, Nakane Chie explains that groups in Japan may be identified by applying two criteria: one is based on the individual's common attribute and the other the individual's position within a given frame. A frame may be a locality, an institution, or a particular relationship that unites a set of individuals in a group. In all cases, it indicates a criterion that defines a boundary and gives a common basis to a set of individuals who are located or involved in it (Nakane, 1970). In contrast, attribute refers to being a member of a definite group or caste. Attribute may be acquired not only by birth but also by achievement (ibid).

These criteria serve to identify individuals in a certain group, which can in turn be classified within the whole society even though the group may or may not have a particular function of its own as a collective body (ibid). Within this framework, this chapter deals with certain important elements of social stratification in Japan. Just like many other societies, stratification is based on gender, income, education, and ethnicity. Although there are other distinctions, I focus on these because they are the most relevant for this book.

Gender Inequality

Chapter three described the role of Japanese women in the family, whereas this chapter describes the role of women in society and how society views women and some factors that hinder gender equality in Japan. The fact that Japan is a very male-oriented society finds its roots in Confucian philosophy.

While the Meiji restoration promised a new start for Japanese women, it did not actually improve their position. Women were taken into the industrialization and modernization process and were used as a source of cheap labor. The transformation from a feudal society into an industrial capitalist society resulted in various changes in attitude that lead to riots and strikes. These changes in attitude influenced the position of women and gave birth to various women's movements in Japan, which began as a strong protest against the miserable position of women during the Meiji era. I fact, Christians inspired the early feminist movements in Japan, (see chapter ten).

Contemporary Japanese women have many rights including the rights to vote, to equal education, and to work. But still deep within the heart of society, there are cultural biases and hidden ideas about women that are rooted in the cultures of the Tokugawa and Meiji periods. How does society view and treat unmarried women, widows, and divorced women? Society views divorced women as being strange, weak, and childish. Even if the man misbehaves, the woman is blamed and made to feel ashamed (Meyvis and Walle, 1989). The law bans gender discrimination and proclaims equal rights for men and women, but these laws are only on paper and do not affect real-life situations.

Gender inequality is visible in educational attainment and the labor market. At the 2014 World Economic Forum, Japan ranked 104 out of 136 countries when it comes equal rights. Tradition and discrimination contribute to the finding. Evidence shows that women's chances for advancement are poor. Many Japanese women work below their potential, thus they prefer staying at home.[1] In other cases, working women are told not to get pregnant for a while and in case of pregnancy some of them become victims of bullying and harassment. This is called *Matahara* aka 'maternity harassment'. As a victim of *Matahara* herself, Sayaka Osakabe has been speaking up on behalf of pregnant women and young mothers who are harassed at work.

Lastly, in some companies, when a woman becomes over 24 years old, she is expected to look for a husband, look after her family, and fulfill her duties as a wife. In some cases, the president or boss of a company may advise a young woman to start her own family and even help her find a suitable husband. Gender inequality is culturally rooted and Japan is no exception.

Income & Unemplyment

Japan, which has long regarded itself as being the most egalitarian industrialized nation, is seeing a widening gap between the rich and the poor that is caused by extensive economic and social changes. Whereas once everyone was treated more or less equally, now due to factors such as longer life spans, women in the workforce, and pay based on performance rather than seniority, there is often a stark contrast between the wealthy and the poor. This increasing income stratification raises potentially troubling questions for

---

1 - Japan: Housewife or Businesswoman - does the country need new role models? (Deutche Welle) http://www.dw.de/japan-housewife-or-businesswoman-does-the-country-need-new-role-models/av-18275608

Japan. Sameness, or at least the perception of it, greatly contributes to the social harmony that the Japanese people have historically prized. Government officials privately concede that greater income disparity is inevitable as the economy becomes more competitive, but they fear that differences between the rich and the poor will lead to more theft, petty crime, and a host of other social problems. However, the disparities that exist between the classes in Japan are far less pronounced than those in the US and the UK. A typical chief executive of a large Japanese company earns roughly US$350,000 a year, while an average worker's salary is around US$56,000. By comparison, the average compensation in 1998 for chief executives at the 500 largest US companies was about US$8 million (Storm, 2000). Income inequality also stems from the level and rank of jobs people do. Gender also plays an important role in generating inequality of income and assets in Japan.

Unemployment is another growing problem in Japan. In 2014, unemployment rate was 3.5%.[2] Unemployment Rate in Japan averaged 2.71% from 1953 until 2014, reaching an all time high of 5.60% in July of 2009 and a record low of 1% in November of 1968.[3] Statistics also reveal a high unemployment rate among young people. In 2013, unemployment rate among 25 years old and younger was 6.1%.[4] One reason for this is that the number of young people who voluntarily quit their jobs is increasing. This is due to the difficulty that young graduates experience in finding satisfying jobs in an extremely harsh employment environment in which employment opportunities are quite limited.

Older workers who have been forced to leave their jobs before the normal retirement age as part of corporate restructuring programs find it extremely difficult to find another job. Among those above the retirement age of 60, there is a growing gap between their strong desire to work and employment opportunities. Being unemployed does not just cause financial hardship, it can also lead to health problems. For

---

2 - http://countryeconomy.com/unemployment/japan
3 - http://www.tradingeconomics.com/japan/unemployment-rate
4 - http://countryeconomy.com/unemployment/japan

example, being unemployed leads to lower self-esteem and a loss of connection with society. It can even give rise to crime and instability in society.

Education

The Japanese educational system has generated a lot of debate among scholars and educators. Some praise it, while others criticize it. Some believe that the strong emphasis on the group and unity leads to the individual aspects of a child being ignored. Others suggest that the highly authoritarian educational system can frustrate children. Some suggest that this may even lead to suicide.

Once students have been accepted into a school, the Japanese very skillfully avoid overt competition among them and downplay differences in ability. In fact, almost no one fails. However, the ruthless entrance examinations represent competition at its worst and they cast a shadow far in advance. They subject students to severe pressure throughout most of their schooling and distort the content of their education. Much of the training in senior high schools is devoted not to learning as such, but to preparing students to pass university entrance examinations (Reischauer and Craig, 1989).

On the other hand, some believe that the Japanese education system is unique and teaches children about the importance of unity, harmony, and discipline; we call this moral education. In Japan, going to school is not just about acquiring knowledge; Japanese education emphasizes moral education such as diligence, endurance, deciding to do hard things, wholehearted dedication, and cooperation. For example, children are organized into cleaning groups that have to cooperate to keep their school clean. Physical education is also very important. School children have to exercise every morning.

The Japanese educational system is group oriented and the cohesion of the group is more important than individual competition in classes. Therefore, students are discouraged from asking their teachers many questions because they may be perceived as disrupting the group for their own personal interests. The group is also emphasized over the individual in sport.

How do the school a person attends and the university they graduate from affect stratification in Japan? This is simple to explain. The school or university a person graduates from affects the sort of job they can get and the company or institution they can work at. For instance, it is very prestigious to graduate from Tokyo University. Graduates from this university have many advantages over graduates from other universities: many state employees and high-ranking politicians are Tokyo University graduates.

Normally, companies have a relationship with schools and universities from which they recruit their employees. Recruitment into big companies and government is based on examinations. Many prestigious companies and government institutions invite only candidates from more prestigious universities and colleges to take recruitment examinations. This increases the pressure on students to enter prestigious universities since it will determine the status and rank students will achieve in Japanese society for their entire lives. The most prestigious university is Tokyo University, which is followed by Keio and Waseda Universities and then by the national universities of each prefecture.

Minorities in Japan

Japan has five major minority groups: *burakumin* (a caste-like group), Okinawans (an indigenous race), Ainu (an indigenous race), Japanese-born Koreans, and migrant workers from other countries. The discrimination that many of these groups encounter has its origins in the imperialist and feudal periods in Japan's history. In the 8th century, the Japanese expanded their territory into the lands of the Ainu and Okinawans, two indigenous races whose lands have now been incorporated into modern Japan.

Discrimination dating from Japan's feudal period also exists against outcasts known as *buraku*. Up until now, there have been no buraku and only one Ainu in the Diet, Japan's national parliament. Korea was under Japanese control for 35 years. During World War II, Japanese soldiers forced many Korean women into sexual slavery. Migrant workers moved to Japan in search of a better life but they have faced a great deal of discrimination from Japanese employers, the government, and Japanese nationals. Many of these minority groups have been affected by *doka seisaku*, a Japanese expression that describes a national policy to make the lifestyles and ideologies of the people in its colonies conform to its own.

Japan has also followed a peculiar dual policy in regard to minority groups—forcing assimilation into the cultural mainstream on the one hand and developing measures to segregate them on the other. Sugimoto Yoshio writes, "In every day life, racism and ethnocentrism still remain strong in many sections of the community and establishment" (Sugimoto, 2003). Japan's racial and ethnic homogeneity go hand in hand with Japan's belief that 'Japaneseness' has superior qualities and should not be contaminated (ibid).

As mentioned above, the Japanese population is aging and the birth rate has dropped drastically. Therefore, Japan faces a critical dilemma: should its people mix with other races or not? Will Japan survive this crisis?

Burakumin

The term *burakumin* ('hamlet people') refers to Japan's traditional 'unclean' caste, which is also known as *eta* ('filthy mass') and *hinin* ('nonhuman'). During the Tokugawa period, *burakumin* were forced to live in separate villages and perform society's dirty jobs, which included grave digging, butchery, executions, and other abhorrent jobs. Almost 2% of Japanese people are *buraku* and despite being racially identical to other Japanese people, they are frequently discriminated against. Trapped in a vicious cycle of prejudice and poverty, many *buraku* are forced to fabricate 'clean' family histories. This class was officially abolished in a parliamentary act of 1871, but it is common for an employer to check an applicant's background for *buraku* heritage. Protective parents often employ private detectives to check whether their child's potential spouse has any *buraku* or Korean blood.[5]

---

5 - http://www.japanfortheuninvited.com/articles/burakumin.html

Igarashi Terumi, a member of the *buraku* caste, described her treatment as inhuman when she writes, "I was first told of my *buraku* origins when I was seven years old, not by my parents, but by a non-*buraku* child. At school, other children taunted me with 'You are dirty!', 'You smell!', 'Don't come near me!' They tied my hands behind my back, put worms and snakes on me, and threw rocks at me when I tried to run away from their cruelty." She found it very difficult to find employment. She said, "I took a job with a company where I continued to experience discrimination. My supervisors declared that I was poorly educated and had no ability. My colleagues would talk behind me saying, 'Her blood is different.' 'She eats different food!' 'She is a fool!' 'They have eye diseases!' Unable to handle such treatment, I moved from job to job" (Francis and Nakajima, 1991). These are some interesting statistics about *burakumin*: almost 8% of *burakumin* have incomes below the minimum income necessary for survival, 12% have incomes below the minimum taxable income, and 90% of *burakumin* have incomes lower than the average national income (Meyvis and Walle, 1989).

Ainu and Okinawans

The Ainu are the aborigines of northern Japan. They have been discriminated against for more than a millennium by Japan's central government, which annexed their territories. Throughout history, they have been considered as savages. They have lost their original language. Still, the Japanese government has not acknowledged the Ainu as the indigenous people of Japan or given them the level of financial and moral support that indigenous people receive in other industrialized societies (Sugimoto, 2003).

The case of Okinawans is similar to the Ainu. Okinawa is the southernmost prefecture of Japan and the main island of the Ryukyu archipelago. Because Okinawa had been the semi-independent Ryukyu Kingdom until 1879, Okinawa has a different culture and language from the rest of Japan. Many Japanese people consider Okinawans as foreigners and outsiders. This makes it difficult for Okinawans to find jobs in other areas of Japan and they miss out on other opportunities in life.

Koreans

There are approximately 600,000 North and South Koreans in Japan today. Most of them were born and grew up in Japan. Many of them belong to families who have lived in Japan for three or even four generation. However, since Japanese nationality is based on lineage, these Korean descendants are not automatically awarded Japanese citizenship. This is very hard to understand from a western perspective. A third or fourth generation African in Europe or the US is automatically a citizen. This is not the case in Japan where it is generally the case of 'once a Korean, forever a Korean'. There are also Koreans who have naturalized and some children of Korean–Japanese intermarriages have become Japanese nationals too.

Less than 1% of the approximately 127 million people in Japan are either North or South Korean nationals or Japanese nationals of Korean descent; this contradicts the claims that Japan is a completely homogeneous society. The majority of Koreans are in Japan due to Japanese colonization of Korea. After the annexation of Korea in 1910, Koreans were forced to become the subjects of Imperial Japan. Japanese colonial policy exercised severe control in Korea. In the 1920s and 1930s, Japan used Korean soil to produce rice for export to Japan. This caused severe famine and poverty in Korea. Many Koreans were desperate to escape this poverty and went to Japan in search of jobs.

Between 1939 and 1945, many Koreans were brought to Japan by force to work in hard and inhumane conditions. For instance, many young Korean women were brought to Japan to serve as 'comfort women'. These women had to sexually satisfy Japanese military personnel. After Japan was defeated by the Allied forces in 1945, many Korean women lost face even in their own country of Korea, especially the women who had been used as comfort women. They had no place to go but to stay in Japan and learn to live with their circumstances.

Today, over 60 years later, the Koreans, who are Japan's largest minority group, still have not been socially accepted. The Koreans in Japan have occasionally been viewed as 'problems' by Japan's sensationalist mass media and have yet to be recognized as close neighbors who created and nurtured a unique ethnic culture.

There are many reasons for this discrimination. Koreans are considered inferior. Ethnic relationships between Japanese and Koreans in Japan are still very poor. The Korean minority suffers discrimination in jobs, social welfare, housing, education, and social acceptance. There are many elderly Koreans who live alone and struggle daily to survive. The inability to access even basic welfare has left many Koreans destitute of resources in their senior years. Koreans in Japan are ineligible for benefits from the Japanese government and women are in a particularly perilous predicament if they have no close family who can support them.

Interestingly, many Korean Christian churches in Japan fill this gap and provide services and support to the Korean community in Japan. Also, the church in Japan has been very active in the area of social concerns. Many Korean pastors and missionaries serve the Christian church in Japan; many of these churches are also attended by Japanese Christians. In big cities such as Tokyo, there are many international churches where Koreans, Africans, and other ethnic groups worship alongside fellow Japanese Christians.

Migrant Workers

There are approximately two million foreign residents in Japan. This figure includes Koreans and Chinese. During the 1980s and 1990s, many foreign workers from developing countries, such as the Philippines, Brazil, Peru, and Thailand, came to Japan to find work. They came to Japan to do the jobs that the average Japanese man and woman did not want to do—dirty (*kitanai*) and difficult jobs like washing the deceased and working as construction laborers, and dangerous (*kiken*) jobs such as working in factories. Immigrant women often work as hostesses, house cleaners, strippers, and as workers in the sex industry. There is perhaps much truth in minority groups' claim that their problems result from distortion and prejudice on the part of the Japanese majority. Until 1995, Japan was one of the few nations that had not ratified the International Convention on the Elimination of All Forms of Racial Discrimination that the United Nations brought into existence in 1960 (Sugimoto, 2003).

Japanese discrimination may be rooted in cultural beliefs. Prejudice considers whatever is from the outside (*soto*) as being unclean and underdeveloped. The Japanese have many cultural sayings that are loaded with prejudices. The Japanese cannot accept other ethnicities into their inner circle or treat them as equals to Japanese. As long as a foreigner is a guest (whether at home, in the workplace, or elsewhere in Japan) they will generally be treated in a friendly manner by the Japanese. However, once a foreigner tries to be more than a guest, the attitude of Japanese people toward them often changes drastically, becoming insensitive, cold, and unwelcoming. The Japanese have a saying *gaijin kusai*, which literally means reeking like a foreigner!

Nikkeijin (South American)

In the nineties, Japan had an industrial labor shortage, so the Japanese government made an effort to attract foreign workers. In order to avoid cultural clashes as much as possible, the government gave priority to people of Japanese descent. Also known as *Nikkeijin*, these people were primarily Brazilian, but also other Latin American *Nikkeijin* of up to three generations (sansei). Unlike regular foreign workers, these *Nikkeijin* did not have to possess special skills and were allowed to work in any sector. It was more or less a visa for permanent residence (Hirata and Warschauer, 2013).

Many *Nikkeijin* from Brazil came to Japan to take on temporary (*haken*) positions in the automotive and electronics industries. In 2008, there were 300,000 Brazilians in Japan, making them Japan's third-largest minority after Koreans and Chinese. Brazilian *Nikkeijin* performed cheap, unskilled labor in factories, performing the so-called '3K' tasks that most Japanese didn't want to do: the *kitanai* (dirty), *kitsui* (physically hard), and *kiken* (dangerous) (ibid). After the global financial crisis of 2008, Japanese manufacturers cut production and fired temporary workers, especially the *Nikkeijin*. Many Latin

American *Nikkeijin* struggle in their daily lives because of cultural and language differences, and due to housing discrimination, they reside in mid-size factory towns in central Japan, living in company-sponsored housing or public housing developments. The *Nikkeijin* community suffers from many unique social problems (ibid).

Unlike Japanese citizens, who have universal health insurance, many poor Brazilian families in Japan often lack medical coverage. There are also many reports of young crime and gang violence among Brazilian children. The *Nikkeijin* visa program of the nineties was based on the false assumption that people of Japanese descent could assimilate more easily into Japanese society than other foreigners. However, this assumption has proved to be a resounding failure (ibid).

In 2010, the number of Brazilian *Nikkeijin* had dropped to nearly 210,000. They have fled from Japan's recession, with the government repatriation program paying for their exit. Ironically, Brazil is in the midst of an unprecedented economic boom, and some Brazilians are going home to take advantage of new opportunities there (ibid).

New Nikkeijin (Filipinos)

In 2008, the old *Nikkeijin* were replaced by *New Nikkeijin*, who are now in Japan to fill a demographic gap and offer care service to the increasingly senior population group. The *New Nikkeijin* are children born out of wedlock to Japanese men and Filipinas who lived in Japan from the 1980s through the early 2000s. These children are also known as *Nikkei* children. Most of these Filipinas met their Japanese partners while working in the entertainment industry, particularly in bars. Because of the Immigration Control Law in 2005 that restricted the residence of foreigners on entertainment visas, many Filipinas had to return to the Philippines together with their children, leaving their Japanese partners behind (ibid).

In 2008, due to human rights reasons, the Japanese government adjusted the Immigration Law by allowing *Nikkei* to gain Japanese citizenship if their Japanese fathers admit paternity. The number of

New Nikkei Filipinos is estimated to be around 30,000, which also includes the offspring of Philippines-based Filipinas and Japanese male tourists to that country. Once these Filipinos gain Japanese citizenship, they will be able to live in Japan permanently, without any legal restriction; and if they are interested, they can pursue the caregiver profession. *New Nikkeijin* have an advantage over EPA Filipino nurses and caregivers, as they do not have to pass the onerous national nursing or caregiver exam to find permanent employment in Japan's nursing establishments (ibid).

"The recruitment of *New Nikkeijin* from the Philippines for nursing and caregiving is somehow different than the recruitment of the Brazilian *Nikkeijin,* in the sense that the *New Nikkeijin* are recruited by an initiative of the private sector, and they have often sought labor beyond the government-created EPA nursing and caregiver programs. However, the number of *New Nikkeijin* is much smaller that the 210,000 of additional caregivers needed in 2015 than in 2011; and at least 730,000 more will be required by 2025 (ibid).

Chapter Six

Social Concerns

Like any society, Japan has its own set of social and cultural problems. Some of these problems are considered to be unique to Japan. This chapter describes some of these problems to give a picture of what is going on in Japan.

The previous chapters have made it clear that Japan is on the brink of a serious social and cultural transformation. The changing role of women in Japan, the increasing divorce rate, the low birth rate, a fatherless generation, isolated youth, and changing family values are all part of these social transformations. The increasing popularity of digital technology has given rise to other social phenomena, which sometimes lead to extreme social and cultural behavior that result in social problems and moral decay in Japan. This chapter considers three main types of social and cultural problems: (1) sexual; (2) children and youth; and (3) social behavior.

Sexual

The sex industry accounts for 1% of the gross national product, which is equivalent to the defense budget. Despite the rickety economy, the sex industry continues to grow. Most prostitutes come from other countries. There are 60,000–70,000 Filipino dancers in Japan, a third of which are undocumented. Filipino women are vulnerable to trafficking due to the Asian economic crisis.

There was no decline in applications for entertainer visas for Japan in the first six months of 1998. Travel to Japan increased 21% in the first half of 1998 compared with the same period in 1997. The label 'entertainer' sometimes has the connotation 'sex worker.' These women are vulnerable in Japan because they are young and beautiful in a hazardous and vulnerable occupation. Trafficking laws exist but are not enforced.[1]

Pornography

Japan produces 30,000 titles of pornographic videos per year (Bales, 2007). This indicates that Japan has a very active sex industry. Even in the Tokugawa period, erotic and pornographic literature was distributed in Japan. Japan makes 21% of worldwide pornography revenues, which is approximately 20 billion US dollars per year.[2]

Pornography is so pervasive that even school children have access to comic books with pornographic content. Sex magazines can be purchased at vending machines. Pornography is available 24 hours a day through cable television. Pornography can be accessed through computer networks. Advertisements known as 'pink chirashi' promoting videos and massage parlors are placed in people's mailboxes. Japan is one of the world's biggest producers of child pornography. The U.S. State Department's 2013 report on human rights practices in Japan labels the country "an international hub for the production and trafficking of child pornography."[3] – It was only in 2014 that Japan passed child pornography law.

Sekkusu shinai shokogun, or celibacy syndrome

Some believe that because of cybersex and virtual porn, some of Japan's under-40s won't go forth and multiply out of duty, as postwar generations did.[4] Japan's under-40s population, are trying out new form of low-commitment relationship called "pot noodle love," one that announces casual sex and virtual-porn as its constituents. This sort of lifestyle is creating social impotence for many.[5]

---

1 - Fact Book on Global Sexual Exploitation, 1999
2 - http://www.ministryoftruth.me.uk/wp-content/uploads/2014/03/IFR2013.pdf
3 - http://www.independent.mk/articles/6241/Japan+Passes+Child+Pornography +Law#sthash.FDUdqiZ5.dpuf
4 - http://www.theguardian.com/world/2013/oct/20/young-people-japan-stopped -having-sex
5 - http://www.collective-evolution.com/2014/01/16/japans-birth-rates-at-all-time -low-people-are-no-longer-interested-in-relationships/

According to Japanese-American author Roland Kelts, who writes about Japan's youth, the future of Japanese relationships will be largely technology driven. "Japan has developed incredibly sophisticated virtual worlds and online communication systems. Their smart phone apps are the world's most imaginative" (ibid).

Digital Crimes

Late nineties when camera phones became widely available in the US, Japan already had more than 25 million camera phones. Japan leads the world in high-tech mobile phones. However, these phones are used in the social problem of digital crime. Men secretly take photos of women on the streets, at swimming pools, in department stores, etc. Some even sell these pictures or video clips to the sex industry either on the Internet or to video companies.

Many people, even prominent people with high ranks and positions, are addicted to this digital sickness. Japan is not the only nation with this problem. Other Asian countries and even the US are confronted with this problem. Kageyama Kinsuke, a professor in criminal psycho-pathology, believes that this problem is caused by stress. "Many middle-aged men secretly glance at women because they are addicted to their work and do not know how to deal with their stress." According to Kageyama, most men who do such things are respected people in society, but they feel something missing in their lives and they do not feel important in their organizations. "Perhaps they are trying to create a feeling of satisfaction by secretly filming other people. This act gives them a false feeling of ruling/controlling someone" (Duits, 2002).

According to Kamon Hei, a journalist at *Asahi Shinbun*, a Japanese newspaper, about 20% of Japanese pornographic videos are filmed by secret cameras (ibid). Japan has very weak laws concerning using secret camera to take photographs; the fine for this crime is approximately US$600. The situation is very different in the US. According to a CNN report, secretly photographing or filming a woman may lead to a $100,000 fine and imprisonment in the US.

Groping

In Japan, more than 4,000 men are arrested each year for groping women on trains. *Chikan* is someone who commits continual public acts of molestation, such as groping on a crowded Japanese train. It is estimated that between 50 to 70% of young women in Japan experience *chikan* on Japanese commuter trains in metropolitan areas (Burgess & Horii, 2012). Gropers molested 2,201 women in 2004. High school girls are the main targets and the lines they use are the ones favored by molesters. Various tactics have been used to stop the assaults, including putting plainclothes women police officers on to trains.[6]

Underage Sexual Relationships

A growing number of schoolgirls in Japan are turning to prostitution so that they can afford expensive designer items such as $500 Prada purses or $350 Louis Vuitton wallets. Tokyo Metropolitan University sociologist, Miyadi Shinji, estimates that 8% of school girls in Japan and one third of all girls who do not go to college, join the sex industry. Furthermore, men are turning to increasingly younger girls.

One factor that contributes to the increase in school girl prostitution is that health officials do not express much concern about the rates of AIDS and other sexually transmitted diseases in the population. Admittedly, the number of cases of AIDS, HIV, and venereal disease in Japan are fairly low, but some health officials believe that these diseases may be underreported because many people are not tested for them. "There is a possibility that many more teenagers are carriers and aren't reflected in the statistics," said Kato Taku, director of an AIDS research team at the Ministry of Health.[7] Teen prostitution is not shocking news. The age limit for sex is 13. These kinds of practices imply that Japan is on the edge of an increasing degeneration of morals and ethics in all facets of life.

---

6 - http://www.telegraph.co.uk/news/worldnews/asia/japan/1483150/
    Record-number-of-women-groped-on-Tokyos-subway.html
7 - www.aegis.com

Children & Youth Issues

Youth in Japan are subjected to huge pressures. High expectations from parents, difficulties at home, hard standards of schooling, and the prospect of losing face when failing at school cause many youth to become stressed, depressed, and even suicidal. Many end up spending many years in self-imposed isolation. Below are some problems that are causes for concern.

Bullying

Bullying is a common problem in every generation and every country. In Japan, it is a relatively serious social problem. Actually, the amount of bullying (*ijime*) in Japan has been decreasing. However, bullying has been becoming increasingly more sinister. In 1994, Okochi Kiyoteru, a 13-year-old junior high school student, committed suicide to escape being bullied by his classmates. This incident received extensive media coverage. The note he left stated that he had been a victim of cruel bullying. He was often forced to soak his face in a dirty river. His bicycle was repeatedly broken and his classmates even demanded that he bring money to them every day. The amount of money that he gave to the bullies reached about $10,000. This was not the first time that a student had committed suicide because of bullying, but it was the first time that the Japanese media gave extensive coverage to *ijime*. Subsequently, bullying became a serious topic in Japan. People wondered why his classmates bullied him. There are many possible reasons, but none of the causes is simple.

Unlike the US where bullying traditionally entails one or two strong students threatening a larger number of weaker students, bullying in Japan usually takes the form of a large group of students picking on or tormenting one or two weaker ones. The victims have nowhere to go. There is little professional help available for victims of bullying in Japan and victims often refuse to seek such help because they fear losing face. Fitting into a group is very important in Japan. Bullying sometimes ends with the victim committing suicide. After the suicide, there is a massive display of grief by the school and classmates who almost all deny that they knew that was anything wrong, which is often not true. They knew about it but due to fear and cultural constraints, they do not want to reveal the true story.

Child Abuse

In 2000, the government passed the Child Abuse Prevention Law; it has been revised twice, once in 2004 and once in 2005. Since the government started collecting data in 1990, the number of reported cases of child abuse increased from 1,101 to 10,000 in 1999 and to 40,000 in 2007 (Kingston, 2010). According to Kingston:

> *"This sudden sharp increase reflects the growing scale of the problem, changing attitudes towards what constitutes abuse, the prolonged economic malaise, and legally mandated reporting on the part of teachers, counselors, doctors, and police. Yet reported cases represent only the tip of the iceberg as many victims and their families remain reluctant to involve the authorities. This reflects not only the fear of social stigma, but also low levels of awareness and a lack of adequate counseling facilities" (ibid).*

Child abuse is mostly committed by mothers, especially single mothers in urban communities who are outside their community settings and away from their relatives and family members. Kingston suggests that the decline in three-generation households, a lack of public care facilities for infants and preschool children, and increasing rates of poverty contribute to the increase in abuse and violence against children. He also suggests that many parents may have been harshly treated as children and that they in turn treat their children using the patterns of discipline and punishment that they grew up with. Social norms are changing in Japan, as elsewhere, and what once passed as acceptable is now considered abusive; the legacies of past abuse linger (ibid).

Hikikomori

As mentioned earlier, *hikikomori* is a serious problem in Japan. *Hikikomori* basically means the self-imposed isolation of a person, normally a young person, from society and family. Hikikomori has even entered the Oxford English Dictionary as "In Japan: abnormal avoidance of social contact". They lock themselves up in a room and often do not come out for years, sometimes even decades. The average age of *hikikomori* also seems to have risen over the last two decades. Before it was 21 - now it is 32.[8]

Hikikomori are seen as predominantly among male. Some suggest that males occupy 70%- 80% of the group. However, an Internet survey by NHK found just 53% to be male. Female withdrawal into the home seems so natural to Japanese society that it may remain unreported, speculates Andy Furlong at the University of Glasgow.[9] Andy Furlong, an academic at the University of Glasgow relates the growth of the *hikikomori* phenomenon with the popping of the 1980s "bubble economy" and the start of Japan's recession of the 1990s. It is estimated that the number of people now affected is 200,000, but a 2010 survey for the Japanese Cabinet Office came back with a much higher figure - 700,000. Since sufferers are by definition hidden away, Tamaki Saito, a psychiatrist, places the figure higher still, at around one million.[10]

Social behavior

There are also various phenomena that do not affect just the youth but all facets of society. I place these phenomena in the category of social behavior. Below are some examples that affect Japanese society in a negative way.

Gambling Addiction

Pachinko is a very popular slot machine in Japan. There are about 20,000 *pachinko* parlors with an average of 250 machines. The annual income of *pachinko* parlors is approximately 230–270 billion US dollars. This is comparable with the total gross national product

---

8 - http://www.bbc.com/news/magazine-23182523
9 - http://www.bbc.com/news/magazine-23182523
10 - Ibid.

of Belgium and it exceeds the combined income of all Japanese car manufacturers (Duits, 2002). Approximately 1.25 million Japanese are addicted to *pachinko*. *Pachinko* players and addicts come from various backgrounds but stressed salarymen and single mothers tend to dominate.

Suicide

Comparing to the year 2008, suicide rate is slightly dropped from 32,249 people to 27,283 in 2013.[11] In 2008, more young people are committing suicide than in the past; 2008 marked the highest number of suicides (4,850) among people in their 30s since the government began compiling detailed statistics in 1978. Due to the stigma of suicide experts believe that the number of deaths ascribed to suicide is an underestimate (Kingston, 2010). Officials determined the cause of suicide in only about two thirds of the cases in 2008. The ranking of reasons for committing suicide in cases where this can be determined has been relatively stable during the Heisei era; for 2008, it was: health problems (65%), financial problems (32%), family problems (17%), and work problems (10%). Depression is the most commonly cited health problem, accounting for 43% of the cases in which health problems were cited. The highest incidence of depression-related suicides occurred among those in their 30s. According to Kingston:

> *There are three powerful factors that explain the high rate of suicide in Japan and why it has stayed persistently high since the mid-1990s. The prolonged economic malaise, the rapidly aging society, and inadequate diagnosis and treatment of mental depression are the major causes of suicide in Japan. For middle-aged salarymen, a loss of job or other significant economic setback makes it difficult to provide for their families. Although insurance companies have extended the waiting period between when a life insurance policy is purchased and when it comes into effect, essentially aimed at addressing the costly problem of*

---

11 - Japan National Police Agency report 2013: http://www.npa.go.jp/safetylife/seianki/jisatsu/H25/H25_jisatunojoukyou_01.pdf

clients committing suicide shortly after enrolling, suicide does not invalidate the policy (ibid).

Homeless People

The number of homeless people is increasing. They live on the streets, in stations, in public parks, and besides rivers. In central Tokyo, the number of homeless has nearly doubled to about 5,000 in 2007 from 3,200 in 1998. Osaka The city has Japan's largest homeless population of 7,700 officially, or more than 10,000 unofficially. However it is still rare to see people sleeping on the street.[12]

The average age of Japan's homeless is 55.9 years old. Experts say that ingrained cultural attitudes about age exacerbate the problem. The problem has become so prevalent that Doctors Without Borders—a nongovernmental health organization accustomed to missions in the poorest of nations—sent staff to this high-tech, high-rise capital (Kambayashi, 2004).

The first-ever nationwide survey found 25,296 homeless people in Japan. However, the actual figure is likely to be much higher according to those working with the homeless. About two thirds of that number are between 50 and 64. Moreover, about 55% of them used to work in construction. Many were day laborers who toiled without fringe benefits to help Japan flourish in the postwar era. But the recession hit contractors hard (ibid).

In Japan, not only the homeless but also people over 35 have difficulty finding a job, especially if they are unmarried. Companies expect married men to work more strenuously since husbands are usually the sole breadwinners. That is why most of the homeless are middle-aged or older single men—a unique aspect of the problem of homelessness in Japan activists say. Most of the homeless are systematically ostracized from society. Japan's homeless problem is attributed to deeply rooted discrimination. Those who look after

---

12 - International Network of Street Papers: http://www.street-papers.org/
case-studies-asia/ (accessed on 21 August, 2014)

homeless people say that homeless people suffer from low self-esteem and feelings of inadequacy and that age discrimination reinforces their sense of alienation (ibid).

Japanese society is changing rapidly and it faces serious sociological, cultural, and moral challenges. Families are under considerable pressure while women, children, and minorities are vulnerable groups in society. Moral problems are increasing rapidly and becoming more complex. Social problems such as *hikikomori* are phenomena of modern high-tech Japanese society. The following chapter analyzes Japanese society and presents some conclusions. In particular, it describes effective strategies for how to reach Japan with the gospel of Jesus Christ.

RELIGION

IN **JAPAN**

PART **THREE**

Chapter Seven

Main Religions in Japan

Prior to studying the religions of Japan, it is important to consider how the Japanese view religion in general. There are essentially two categories of religion in Japan: revealed and natural religions. Buddhism, Christianity, Islam, and some new religions are considered revealed religions because they have specific books and scriptures that provide guidelines for life and religious rituals. In contrast, natural religions are more traditional and based on folklore; they have few or no books or scriptures. Even though Shintoism does have some texts and scriptures, it is considered to be more a natural religion.

It is important to emphasize that when people talk about religion in Japan they generally mean revealed religions, particularly Christianity. When Japanese people say that they are non-religious, they mean they are not committed to a revealed religion or religious organization. Japanese people often view all religions as a single entity rather than as distinct religions. It is often said that the Japanese are born Shintoist, have a Christian (western) style wedding, and die Buddhist (as many Japanese have Buddhist funerals). Japanese do not feel compelled to be committed to a particular organized religion. This mindset is called *mushukyo* in Japanese, which means "no religion" or "non-religious."

It is crucial to understand the characteristics of *mushukyo*. First, being non-religious does not mean that one does not believe in gods or *kami*, but rather that one does not believe in an organized religion. The Japanese consciously or unconsciously separate these two things. Religion is understood in a Western–Christian framework, and thus folkloric or indigenous festivals known as *matsuri*, which are related to Shinto and sometimes Buddhist culture, are not considered religious. This makes the Japanese religious mind more complex and difficult to understand for outsiders. This is better understood when we distinguish between religion and religious culture. Japanese can participate in religious culture without being a part of an organized revealed religion. To a certain degree, this can be true in Western European societies as well. For instance, one may celebrate Christmas in many Western countries without being religious or belonging to an organized church. Pentecost is a national holiday in the Netherlands; some people celebrate this event without being a part of a church or a Christian denomination. Some may not even know what the meaning of the day really is.

Further, *mushukyo* does not mean that the Japanese do not have religious sentiments. This is visible in the way the Japanese honor their ancestors on *Obon* day or visit Shinto shrines and temples during at New Year. Japanese are actually relatively engaged when it comes to religious sentiments and even religious superstitions. Why do the Japanese prefer to be nonreligious? According to Ama Toshimaro, professor at Meiji Gakuin University in Tokyo and the author of *Why are the Japanese Non-Religious?* (*Nihonjin wa naze mushukyo nanoka* in Japanese), annual festivals such as *Obon* and other cultural festivals are a means of gaining spiritual peace and replace the need for Western-style organized religion. There is thus no need for people to choose revealed religions as their means of spiritual liberation (Ama, 2005).

According to Ama, incidents and scandals surrounding religious organizations further contribute to the unpopularity of organized religions. Reports that some religious groups deceive their members into making large donations and organizing supernatural events make most Japanese uncomfortable with organized religions. Another reason why Japanese may feel suspicious about organized religions is the widely held perception that such religions are detrimental to the public peace. For instance, Japanese disapprove of Christians who walk in the streets with megaphones calling people sinners and asking them to repent. This is not acceptable to most Japanese. Even though the majority of Christians do not perform such acts, Japanese people are often cautious of Christianity because of its evangelical wing (ibid).

Lastly, the exclusive nature of some aspects of revealed religions cause people to shun them. Those who are already members of a religion enjoy reading holy texts, praying, and singing songs, but these are often not pleasant experiences for an outsider. In his book, Ama indicates that unless one becomes aware of the importance of life and its related anxieties, revealed religion does not make sense (ibid). This awareness is often created when one realizes how irrational life can be; it can lead a person to seek answers in revealed religions, but the Japanese generally prefer to be *mushukyo* (ibid). Shinto and Buddhism are Japan's two main religions alongside Confucianism. These three religions have coexisted for several centuries. They complement each other to a certain degree.

Religion does not play a major role in the everyday life of most Japanese people today. The average person typically observes religious rituals at ceremonies associated with births, weddings, and funerals. They may visit a shrine or temple on New Year's Day and participate in local festivals, *matsuri*, most of which have a religious background.

Shinto

Shinto is the indigenous faith of the Japanese people and is as old as Japan itself. It remains one of the two main religions in Japan (the other is Buddhism). Shinto means 'the way of the gods.' Unlike Christianity and Islam, it does not have a founder or sacred scriptures. Proselytization and preaching are not common either because Shinto is deeply rooted in the Japanese people and their traditions. Shinto gods are called *kami*. They are spirits that take the form of objects and concepts important for life such as wind, rain, mountains, trees, rivers, and fertility. Humans become *kami* after they die and are revered by their families as ancestral *kami*. The sun goddess, Amaterasu, is considered Shinto's most important *kami*. In contrast to most monotheistic religions, there are no absolutes in Shinto. It has no concept of absolute right and wrong or of absolute good and evil.

During the Meiji period, people were encouraged to believe and practice Shinto because it was strongly associated with emperor worship. In Shinto belief, the emperor is a god or a *kami* who is a lawful descendent of Amaterasu, the founding goddess of Japan.

From the earliest times until now, the principal objects of worship in Shinto are the divinities known as *kami*. A literal translation of the word kami is 'that which is hidden.' *Kami* are venerated and worshipped. They include animals, birds, mountains, grass, and trees as well as historical and mythical figures. *Kami* may be good or evil. Hence, Shinto *kami* include dragons, foxes, tigers, and tree spirits.

During the Tokugawa period, Shinto was subordinate to Buddhism. However, people gradually became distrustful of Buddhism due to the corruption of Buddhist priests. In the Meiji Restoration, Shinto became the national religion of Japan. This 'State Shinto' has a strong ethnocentric belief that Japan is the most superior nation in the world. Shinto believes that the Japanese emperor is a god who is to be worshipped. After World War II, this form of Shinto was banned and the emperor renounced his deity.

There are three kinds of Shinto—Shrine Shinto, Sect Shinto, and Folk Shinto. Shrine Shinto is the oldest form of Shinto and has the largest number of followers. It involves worshiping *kami* at local shrines. Such worship has exerted a unifying effect on Japanese society. While Shinto has no founder, it possesses an organization based on believers, festivals, religious practices, doctrines rooted in Shinto traditions, and Japanese myths. All these are centered on shrines and spiritual unification (Naofusa, 1987).

Sect Shinto is not as common as Shrine Shinto. It is a new form of Shinto: 13 sects were founded in the 19th century. These groups generally do not have shrines but instead use churches as centers for their religious activities (ibid). These are so-called new religions and are characterized by shamanistic leadership and philosophical beliefs.

Folk Shinto is very popular among lower income classes in Japan. It does not have any official teachings or social organization. Rather, it has three sources: (1) ancient traditions such as divination, shamanistic rituals, and folk medicine; (2) basic elements such as customs of abstinence and purification rites as well as worship of house and field *kami*; and (3) syncretism of Shinto with beliefs from foreign religions such as Buddhism, Taoism, and Christianity.

What are the main beliefs of Shinto? Originally, Shinto possessed no theology or ethics beyond an abhorrence of death and defilement and an emphasis on ritual purity. Shinto creation stories relate the history and lives of the *kami*. Among them was a divine couple, Izanagi no mikoto and Izanami no mikoto who gave birth to the Japanese islands. Their children became the deities of the various Japanese clans. Amaterasu Omikami, the sun goddess, was one of their daughters. She is the ancestress of the Imperial Family and is regarded as the chief deity. Her shrine is at Ise. Her descendants unified the country. Her brother, Susano, came down from heaven and roamed throughout the earth. He is famous for killing a great evil serpent.

The *kami* are the Shinto deities. The word *kami* is generally translated 'god' or 'gods.' However, the *kami* bear little resemblance to the gods of monotheistic religions. There are no concepts that are comparable with the Christian concepts of God's wrath, omnipotence, omnipresence, and his separation from humanity due to sin. Numerous other deities are conceptualized in various forms:

- Those related to natural objects and creatures from 'food to rivers to rocks.'
- Guardian kami of particular areas and clans.
- Exceptional people (including all but the last of the emperors).
- Abstract creative forces.[1]

Aspects of Kami

The *kami* are shadowy, formless entities that are largely devoid of personality and resemble impersonal manifestations of power. All *kami* are considered to have superior knowledge and power than people;

they hold in their power those areas of life that lie outside human control. *Kami* have no shape of their own. To manifest themselves, they must be summoned or cajoled into a vessel of suitably inviting form. These vessels are known as *yorishiro* and are frequently long and thin: trees, wands, banners, or long stones are common (Bowring and Kornicki, 1993).

In Japan, dolls are also believed to be residents of *kami*. Also, certain physically gifted people can act as mediums between humans and *kami*. Women mostly act as mediums; a *kami* may borrow a women's body to communicate and reveal things. *Kami* are inherently amoral. They are powers that respond favorably or unfavorably to the human community according to the treatment they receive. Treat them well by performing proper rituals, offerings, and cultic worship and they can be expected to respond with blessings in the form of good rice harvests, flourishing progeny, and protection from fire, famine, and diseases.

However, if you neglect them by exposing them to pollution, they will immediately blast the community with *tatari* or curses (Bowring and Kornicki, 1993). *Kami* dislike pollution. This pollution is not environmental pollution, but spiritual pollution caused by things that are unclean in the natural realm. Anything that is unclean may cause pollution; uncleanness is mainly related to blood, dirt, and death. These things can make objects and people unclean, generating pollution, and thus angering the *kami*.

It is critical to understand that it is not moral sin that makes the *kami* angry but pollution. *Kami* are offended by blood, particularly blood produced at human birth and death and during women's menstruation. Woman's menstruation is called 'red pollution' and women are not allowed to visit shrines when menstruating. Those who have experienced a recent death in the family cannot visit a shrine for a while.

In the Christian faith, the blood of Jesus was shed to forgive the sins of those who believe in him. Is it possible that this blood will also anger the *kami* and consequently the message of the blood of Jesus does not fit within the concept of pollution that Shintoists believe in?

Kami specialize in certain areas—some impart blessings for a good marriage, others for good business, and others for study, etc. Also, in Shintoism, ancestors are highly venerated and some even become *kami*. All of humanity is regarded as *"kami's* child." Thus, all of human life and human nature are regarded as sacred. Believers revere *musuhi,* the *kami's* creative and harmonizing powers. They aspire to have *makoto*, which is sincerity or a true heart. This is regarded as the way or the will of the *kami*. Morality is based on that which benefits the group. "Shinto emphasizes right practice, sensibility, and attitude."[2]

There are four affirmations in Shinto:

1. Tradition and family: The family is seen as the main mechanism by which traditions are preserved. The principal family celebrations relate to birth and marriage.

2. Love of nature: Nature is sacred; to be in contact with nature is to be close to the *kami*. Natural objects are worshipped as sacred spirits.

3. Physical cleanliness: Followers of Shinto frequently take baths, wash their hands, and rinse their mouths.

4. *Matsuri:* Worship and honor are given to the kami and ancestral spirits.[3]

Spirits of the Dead and Life after Death

The Japanese believe in spirits of the dead, which are called *tama*. A *tama* resides in a host and imparts life and energy to it, but it detaches itself during illness and leaves the body permanently at death. It then requires nourishment from the living if it is to achieve a state of rest and salvation. For 33 years, the family of the dead person must observe the correct rituals (*kuyo*): presenting food offerings, visiting the grave, and chanting ritual words. After 33 years, the spirit is believed to lose its individual nature and to merge with its ancestors (Bowring and Kornicki, 1993).

Spirits of the dead that are neglected within these 33 years pose a threat to society. Spirits without any surviving family members are also dangerous. Lastly, spirits of people who die violently, in disgrace, or with anger in their hearts are considered dangerous. These three types of *tama* are believed to wander over the earth and cause disasters and calamities.

In Japan, it is believed that all the dead—irrespective of the moral quality of their lives on earth—assemble at the summits of certain holy mountains. Such mountains have symmetrical shapes and include Mount Fuji and Kiso Ontake. There are shrines at the feet of such mountains where the dead are venerated in rituals. The dead are believed to return from these places during specific seasons to bless their families. These seasons are the New Year and the *bon* festival in August. These annual festivals are seasons for welcoming back the dead.

Shinto and Christianity are quite different. In Christianity, salvation is obtained by believing in Jesus Christ and his death and resurrection. In contrast, Shinto lacks the concept of salvation because it has no notion of sin. Therefore, there is no such thing as judgment in Shinto. In Shinto, life after death is spent in the mountains, whereas in the Christian faith life after death is spent in either heaven or hell. Christians believe in a single triune God, (i.e., one God in three persons), whereas the Shinto pantheon is populated by millions of gods. When telling Japanese people about Jesus, they may wonder which one of the millions of gods he represents.

Buddhism

Buddhism originated in India in the 6th century BC. It consists of the teachings of the Buddha—Siddhartha Gautama. Of the two main branches of Buddhism, Mahayana or 'Greater Vehicle' Buddhism found its way to Japan. Buddhism was imported to Japan via China and Korea in the form of a present from the friendly Korean kingdom of Paekche in the 6th century AD. While the ruling nobles adopted Buddhism as Japan's new state religion, it did not initially spread among the common people due to the complexity of its teachings.

There were a few initial conflicts with Shintoism, but the two religions were soon able to coexist in harmony and they even complement each other.

In 1175, Honen founded the *Jodo* sect or the Pure Land sect. Many people from all different social classes followed this sect since its doctrines were simple being based on the principle that anyone can achieve salvation by firmly believing in the Amida Buddha. In 1224, the *Jodo-Shinshu* sect or the True Pure Land sect was founded by Honen's successor, Shinran. *Jodo* sects have millions of followers today.

In 1191, the Zen sect was introduced from China. According to Zen teachings, self-enlightenment can be achieved through meditation and discipline. Buddhist institutions were once more attacked in the early years of the Meiji period when the new Meiji government favored Shinto as the state religion and tried to separate and emancipate it from Buddhism.

In Japan, 90 million people consider themselves Buddhists. However, Buddhism does not directly affect or influence the everyday life of the average Japanese person. Funerals are generally conducted according to the Buddhist way and many households have a small house altar, known as a *butsudan*, to venerate their ancestors. In this respect, Buddhism is similar to Shinto since ancestors are worshipped in both religions. In fact, while ordinary people are often unaware of this, they refer to their recently deceased relatives as 'Buddhas' or *hotoke* (Hendry, 2004). Buddha means 'enlightened one.'

There are also differences between Buddhism and Shinto, especially when Buddhism was first introduced in Japan. For example, the Buddhist way, which sees the source of all evils as lying within our own minds, is in sharp contrast to Shintoism, which blames external forces for ills. The *kami* of Shinto were viewed as bestowers of material blessings that lie beyond the reach of man and never as revealers of internal or ultimate truth. Most religious devotion in early Shinto seems to have been directed toward obtaining divine favors in this world such as bountiful harvests and protection from famine and disease. There were no traditions in Japan that are comparable to those in Taoism of China, namely of spiritual methods that enable the inner consciousness to comprehend and expand the mode of truth (Bowring and Kornicki, 1993). Buddhism teaches that all Buddhists should follow five precepts:

1. Kill no living thing (including insects).
2. Do not steal.
3. Do not commit adultery.
4. Tell no lies.
5. Do not drink intoxicants or take drugs, (McDowell, 1994).

There are other precepts that apply only to monks and nuns.

These include:

6. Eat moderately and only at the appointed time.
7. Avoid that which excites the senses.
8. Do not wear adornments (including perfume).
9. Do not sleep in luxurious beds.
10. Accept no silver or gold, (Ibid).

Further, Buddhism stresses reverence for the Three Treasures: the Buddha, the 'law' or the teachings in the holy scriptures, sutras, etc., and the religious community which resulted in the formation of monastic communities.

Confucianism

Confucianism is more of a philosophy than a religion. Japanese culture, society, and politics have been strongly influenced by this tradition, which originated in China in the 6th century BC. Confucianism is concerned with how an individual should live in this world based on ethics and values for life. Confucianism does not focus on the journey of the soul to the next life. Kong Fuzi, whose name was westernized by Europeans as 'Confucius,' lived from 551 to 479 BC. Confucius was a minor official who aspired to reform the violent and unstable Chinese society of his time (Bowring and Kornicki, 1993).

Neither Confucius nor his followers claim that he was divine in any sense. While it does not stress metaphysics, Confucianism, like other religions, attempts to define or establish a social ethic, a worldview, a scholarly tradition, and a way of life. Confucius taught that self-enlightenment is achieved through harmony, acceptance of harmonious social hierarchy, and the functioning thereof. Therefore, society should be divided into strata and classes where everyone has a place, a function, and duties to the family, the group, and society. Power and position should not be abused; rather, everyone should obey authorities and the authorities should not use their power corruptly.

Confucianism was imported from Korea to Japan during the 5th century AD. Confucianism played a very important role during the early formation of the Japanese state. During the Tokugawa period with its three centuries of stability and closed borders, Confucianism was used as a political and social worldview to organize the family, society, and the government. While Buddhism was the state religion and fulfilled the spiritual needs of society, Confucianism provided practical ethics to enable society to function. Confucian teachings covered all aspects of society and life beginning with structures and ethics within the family. Obedience of sons to their fathers was a very important ethic. Also, women were given categorized ranks of functions and job descriptions that they had to fulfill during their lifetimes. It seems that during the industrialization that occurred during the Meiji period, in contrast to Buddhism, Confucianism adapted easily and it was even used as an ideology for modernization and development. The influence of Confucianism is so great that some even speak of contemporary Japan as being Confucianized. Scholars debate the extent to which this is true.

I certainly believe that the Confucian emphasis on the family, paternalism, harmony, and hierarchy, in conjunction with Shinto and Buddhism, has profoundly influenced Japanese culture and society today. However, these values and ethics, which are based on

Confucian teachings, are gradually being eroded. Previous chapters considered the family, the role of women, and other aspects of society. The influence of Confucianism is quite apparent in these areas, but changes are occurring, especially in family and working life.

New Religions in Japan

The new religions and their members are important and distinctive groups in Japanese society (Hardcare, 199). The new religions, *shinko shukyo*, were primarily formed during three different periods. The first period occurred in the 1800s, and groups such as the *Tenri-kyo* and *Konko-kyo* were formed at this time. During the second period, which took place in the 1920s, *Gedatsu-kai* (a sect that is a syncretistic blend of Shinto, Buddhism, and Confucianism), *Omoto-kyo*, and *Hito-no-michi* (another Shinto-related sect) were established. The third period took place during the post-World War II era. New religious groups at this time included *Hito-no-michi*, (which later became *PL Kyodan* aka Perfect Liberty Church); *Tensho Kotai Jingo-kyo*, also known as *Odoru Shu-kyo* (the Dancing Religion); and the *AUM Shinrikyo*[4] were founded. It is not really clear how many new religions exist in Japan and how many people are members or have affiliations with such organizations.

The content of the new religions, mainly their doctrines and teachings, are simply popularized versions of Shinto and Buddhism (Thomsen, 1963). Mullins suggests that in a Japanese context, new religions draw from a vast reservoir of beliefs and practices related to ancestors, the spirit world, Buddhism, Shinto, and Confucianism (Mullins, 1998).

However, there is one important new element in the new religions, namely Christianity, or rather Christian doctrines and teachings taken out of their original context and more or less skillfully mixed with tenets from Buddhism and Shinto (Thomsen, 1963).

---

4 - *Asahara Shoko, who launched a nerve gas attack on a Tokyo subway in 1995, led AUM Shinrikyo.* The group later changed its name to Aleph and tried to rehabilitate itself without its founder.

Even though the new religions are all different, one can find some commonalities in their teachings and goals; they emphasize individual prosperity, spiritual healing, societal harmony, and apocalyptic worldviews concerning the end of the world and the establishment of a new world.

New Japanese religions offer followers the possibilities of developing their own spiritual powers that help them to perceive mysterious phenomena. It is believed by scientists that such spirituality and metaphysical desires can be viewed as an expression of the reaction against scientific materialism and increasing rationalism in the modern society (Buckley ed., 2002). The following is written about new religions in the *Encyclopedia of Contemporary Japanese Culture* edited by Sandra Buckley (2002):

> *Many view the established religions of Japan as exhausted and stagnant when faced with the challenges of modern life and turn instead to new religions as an antidote to perceived importance of the older religious traditions. Critical of the failure of the modernity, on the one hand, but aware of the limitations of the pre-modern worldview; on the other, individuals seek for alternatives to address problems of spiritual, social and emotional malaise. Viewed in this light, the Japanese new religions are products of, and impetus for, religious change and dynamism in contemporary Japanese society (Buckley ed., 2002).*

Interestingly, a high number of leaders in new religions are women either acting as founders and/or current leaders. New religions also attempt to reach out to Japanese people abroad as well as those of Japanese descent, for instance, in Latin American countries like Brazil. New religions are very skillful in utilizing the Internet, social media and Manga books for attracting new members.

Islam in Japan

According to an *Operation World* report in 2010, 190,493 Muslims live in Japan, with an annual growth of 1.3% (Mandryk, 2010). An increase of migrant workers, such as factory workers from the Middle East and Southeast Asia, in the 1960s and 70s, led to the growth of Muslim communities in Japan. There are at least 65 mosques and several Islamic organizations in Japan. In addition, some Japanese have converted to Islam because of marriage or personal desire to do so.

Even though the number of Muslims in contemporary Japan is small, Japan has a deep relationship with Islam, especially with political Islam. During the early 1900s, Japan was admired by many Muslim scholars and populist Muslim leaders in Southeast Asia and others within the Islamic world. They believed that Japan was the first non-Western super power that might be able to challenge Western imperialism. From 1900 until 1945, the question that motivated Muslims and some Japanese was whether Japan could be the "Savior of Islam" against Western colonialism (Essenbel, 2011). From the start of the Meiji period, right-wing organizations advocated Japan's rights in Asia, pioneering contacts with Muslims. Japanese government was using the sympathy of the Muslim world as a means to fulfill her imperialistic ambition in Central and Southeast Asia.

In 1938, the Japanese government started to implement its Islamic policy by creating the Greater Japan Islamic League or the *Dai Nippon Kaikyo Kyokai*. This was the official Islamic organization of Japan until the end of World War II (Ibid). Its main purpose was to promote Islamic studies and culture. Thus, the Tokyo Mosque was opened in 1938. On the opening day of the mosque, delegates were invited from various Islamic countries with all expenses covered by the Japanese government. Japanese officials were in attendance to extend an official welcome of the government to their guests (Ibid). After Japan's defeat in 1945, the numerous Islamic institutions were dissolved, since they were accused of collaborating with the Japanese government against the West.

Judaism in Japan

It is not certain exactly how many Jews live in Japan. At present, the Tokyo and Kobe Jewish communities make it possible for Jews of many different backgrounds—teachers of English, visiting business people, itinerant students and travelers, Israeli jewelry dealers, American tourists—to observe festivals and holidays, to keep the Sabbath, and to preserve their ties to the community, their faith, and to one another. By 1895 this community of approximately 50 families was able to dedicate Japan's first synagogue (Kapner and Levine, 2000). During the early to middle 1900s, Kobe was home to 30,000 Jews, predominantly from Russia, Central and Eastern Europe, Germany and the Middle East. The Middle Eastern Jews, known as "Baghdadi Jews," originally came to Kobe from present-day Iraq and Syria, as well as from Yemen, Iran, and other areas in Central Asia and the Middle East. While some emigrated for economic reasons, others responded to changing developments during the 1930s (Ibid). Currently Tokyo has the largest Jewish community in Japan with its own permanent Rabbi.

There are some Japanese who have converted to Judaism, and there is a fascination among the Japanese in regard to Jewish culture and traditions. There are several pro-Jewish groups in Japan, such as the Japan Kibbutz Association (*Nihon Kibutsu Kyokai*), *Makuya*, a pro-Israel Christian group, and Japanese Christian Friends of Israel. For instance, Makuya and Japanese Christian Friends of Israel both believe that the Japanese people are one of the lost tribes of Israel. Various tours have been organized for the members of these groups to visit Israel regularly.

Chapter Eight

A Brief History
of Christianity in Japan

Christianity has a long history in Japan. Mainstream historians believe that Christianity first entered Japan in the 16th century with the arrival of Portuguese to Japan. Other Christian historians believe that Christianity was introduced to Japan much earlier. They believe that Christianity first came to the Far East roughly 1,800 years ago along the Silk Road through China to Nara in central Japan. Ken Joseph is one of the chief proponents of this theory. This chapter discusses both theories and the subsequent development of Christianity in Japan.

Catholic Christians: The Kirishitan Claim

It is widely accepted that Christianity was first introduced to Japan in the mid-16th century. The religion was generally tolerated until the beginning of the 17th century, when the Tokugawa Shogunate (1603–1867) started to persecute its followers. When relations with the West were restored in the mid-19th century, Christianity was reintroduced and it has continued to exist in Japan with varying fortunes.

In 1548, Anjiro, a 36-year-old man, fled Japan after killing someone and boarded a Portuguese ship heading to India. There he met Francis Xavier, a Portuguese priest, who was sent by the king of Portugal as a missionary to Europeans and Indians in Malacca, a Portuguese territory. In the boat, Xavier asked Anjiro, "If I went to Japan, would the people become Christians?" Anjiro replied, "My people would not immediately become Christians, but they would first ask you a multitude of questions, weighing carefully your answers and your claims. Above all, they would observe whether your conduct agrees with your words. If you should satisfy them on these points by suitable replies to their inquiries and by a life above reproach, then, as soon as the matter was known and fully examined, the king (*daimyo*), the nobles, and the educated people would become Christians. Six months would suffice; for the nation is one that always follows the guidance of reason" (Francis and Nakajima, 1991).

These historic words challenged Xavier to introduce Christianity to Japan. However, Anjiro underestimated the time it would take Japan to become a Christian nation: over five centuries have passed and Japan is still not a Christian nation. Anjiro became a Christian and was baptized. The following year (1549), Xavier entered Japan with Anjiro as his interpreter.

Xavier entered Japan during a period when Japan had not yet been unified as a nation. Local lords, *daimyo*, were fighting each other for territory. Some *daimyo* welcomed the Portuguese in order to obtain modern weapons and technology from them to use against their opponents. The territories (*han*) of *daimyo* who welcomed the Portuguese were located in Hizen, Tosa, and Satsuma, Choshu, and other places. Some *daimyo* even commanded all the people in their territories to become Christians. This angered the non-Christian *daimyo* and they began to fight the newly converted Christians and *daimyo*.

Two years after entering Japan, Xavier left Japan for India and recruited missionaries and workers to go to Japan to evangelize the Japanese. Between 1549, when Xavier entered Japan, and 1595, approximately 300,000 Japanese became Christians, of whom 17 were *daimyo* (Best, 1966). This is the conventional and well-accepted theory of how Christianity first came to Japan.

The Church of the East: The Keikyo Claim

A recent discovery in Xian, China, has dramatically altered the historical record of Christianity in China. Asian countries (particularly China and Japan) are considered to be predominately Buddhist countries. With the exception of the Philippines and Korea, there are very limited records of Christians in Asia. As remarkable as it may seem, the oldest Christian site in Asia has been dated to AD 638. This site, which is near the ancient Chinese capital of Xian, has challenged the previous understanding of the role of Christianity in China, Japan, and other Asian countries. The Nestorian Monument, a stone tablet in the city of Xian, was discovered in the 1600s and it is the only record of Christianity in China. Its clear statement that "monasteries abound in a hundred cities" has always been puzzling. This monument, which is often referred to as the 'Rosetta Stone' of Christianity in Asia, was the only indication of this past (Joseph Jr., 2001). According to this alternative theory, Christianity entered Japan long before Francis Xavier's arrival in Japan. This theory has its origin in China.

For thousands of years, a strong trading relationship existed between China and the Middle East centered on the famous Silk Road. The Silk Road covered a vast distance and linked Israel, Turkey, Iraq, Persia (modern day Iran) China, Korea, and Japan. In addition to commercial goods and materials, scientific knowledge, such as medical and architectural knowledge, was exchanged along this trade route. At the same time, various faiths and beliefs also entered China and Far Asia.

One of these faiths was Christianity, which was brought by Nestorian missionaries from the Assyrian Church of the East. The pioneer of this mission was a man from Iran called Alopen, a Persian bishop who founded the Nestorian mission in Chang-an in AD 635 during the T'ang Dynasty. Chang-an, the upper capital, was the center of imperial splendor. Caravans brought traders, jugglers, monks, and pilgrims from Persia and Armenia, and even Antioch and Byzantium. Their strange appearance and outlandish clothes never failed to amuse the Chinese onlookers. Meanwhile, the Chinese had been transported to Central Asia to garrison fortifications across the steppes. In such a setting, Nestorian Christianity first came to China (Lee, 1971). Some even believe that Christianity entered China and later Japan much earlier than even Bishop Alopen. Some studies suggest that Christianity entered China as early as AD 86, the third year of the reign of Yuan He of the Eastern Han Dynasty.

When studying stone carvings of the Eastern Han Dynasty (AD 25–220) belonging to the Eastern Han Stone Carving Museum, a Christian theology professor Wang Weifan was greatly surprised to discover that some stone engravings recorded Bible stories and had designs dating from early Christian times. Some of these engravings were made in AD 86, which is 550 years earlier than the generally accepted time that Christianity entered China. Members of The Church of the East have long believed that the apostle Thomas first brought the gospel to China through India as early at AD 64 and Japan in about AD 70.[1] I do not believe that this indicates that Thomas traveled to Japan himself, but rather that the people and offspring of those he led to Christ in India brought Christianity to China and from China to Japan.

The story of the *keikyo*, the Church of the East, aka the Nestorian Christianity, is very interesting. The Japanese name *Keikyo* (in Chinese *jingjiao*) was used to call this teaching when it came to China and meant the luminous teaching (Kubo, 1999). I personally believe this theory, which claims that Christianity arrived in Japan long before Francis Xavier's time. However, it is up to the reader to decide which claim has the strongest support. For interested readers, there are fascinating books and websites about *keikyo* Christians and the spread of Christianity through Assyrian and Persian missionaries in China and Japan. One such book is *Lost Identity*[2] by K. Joseph Jr. This book presents historical and archaeological evidence that Japan was once a Christian nation and was influenced by Christianity long before Francis Xavier's arrival in the 16th century. He also claims that there were multicultural societies in some parts of Japan. He even claims that some cities such as Kyoto were constructed by immigrants who came to Japan to settle and work. Their cultures and customs mixed with those of the native inhabitants of Japan.

---

1 - www.keikyo.com
2 - This e-book is available for free on the internet at http://www.onmarkproductions.com/ LostIdentity.pdf

Another interesting book is *The Lotus and the Cross* written by S. K. Lee in the early 1970s. Like Joseph, Lee claims that Christianity first came to Japan through Nestorian believers from the Church of the East. He discusses how the Iranian bishops rapidly spread Christianity. He claims that many temples were built for worshiping Christ that were later burned down or destroyed by Buddhists. Finally, the website of the Keikyo Institute (www.keikyo.com) gives a variety of information about early Christianity in Japan.

Which Claim to Believe?

Which claim a person believes may be influenced by their view of Christianity. For example, if a person believes that Catholicism, which is strongly western-oriented with its roots in Southern Europe, is the only form (or a superior form) of Christianity, then that person may prefer to believe that Xavier first brought Christianity to Japan. On the other hand, if Catholicism is considered to be just one form of Christianity and that Christianity is not only a Western faith, but one that originated in the Middle East, then the second claim (the *keikyo* claim) could be a possibility.

Christianity may have entered Japan much earlier than the first Catholic missionaries. Of course, another form of Christianity—Protestantism—subsequently entered Japan during the Meiji period. This is discussed later in this chapter, but before that we consider how Christianity developed during the Tokugawa period.

Christianity During the Tokugawa Period

The first thing Xavier and his companions did when they arrived in Japan was to translate the catechism into Japanese with the help of Anjiro, the man who became a Catholic after he met Xavier on the ship while fleeing Japan because he had committed murder. The missionaries began to preach by reading the Japanese catechism. The first Japanese catechism describes the creation of heaven and earth by God, the fall of the angels, the creation of Adam and Eve, Noah's flood, the construction of the tower of Babel, the beginning of idolatry, the destruction of Sodom, the ugliness of sodomy, the history of Joseph, the son of Jacob, the captivity of the sons of Israel in Egypt and their liberation by Moses, the giving of the Ten Commandments at Mount Sinai, the entrance of the Jews into the promised land, the fall and penance of King David, the prophet Elisha, the preaching of Jonah in Nineveh, Judith and Holofernes, the statue of Nebuchadnezzar, the prophet Daniel, the incarnation, an extensive description of the life and sufferings of the Redeemer, his resurrection and ascension, his return at the last judgment, the reward of the righteous in the everlasting bliss of heaven, and the punishment of the wicked in the eternal torments of hell. Xavier provided an especially detailed description of "the creation of the world and immorality of souls, the necessity of the incarnation of the Divine Word as a remedy of his, the life, sufferings, and death and resurrection and glorious ascension of Christ our Lord" (Higashibaba, 2001).

Xavier and his companion, Fernandez, preached loudly in the streets and told their listeners how the Japanese sinned seriously in three things. First, they had forgotten *Dainichi* or the Almighty God and instead they worshiped the devil in wooden objects, stones, and senseless things. Second, they committed the sin of sodomy, a grievous and hateful sin that caused a great punishment to be inflicted on the world created by the Lord of heaven and earth. Third, the women performed abortion and infanticide to avoid the obligation of rearing children, which was the greatest cruelty and inhumanity (ibid).

However, it is not clear how accurately the catechism was translated or how clearly the message was transmitted to the people. The message Xavier preached challenged almost all aspects of Japanese culture in those days. Despise this, about 300,000 people became Catholic Christians and accepted the message. They developed their own Christian lifestyle in Japan. Soon, some believers were trained to become *dojuku* or assistant priests. In the absence of priests, religious duties were entrusted to *dojuku* who helped at churches and the priests' residences and preached, catechized, and instructed Christians. They did not take religious vows but they shaved their heads and wore a kind of cassock and they devoted themselves to the service of the church (Harrington, 1993).

Persecution and the Hidden Christians (*Kakure Kirishitans*)

Things began to change when politics became involved. Certain *daimyo* tolerated the Catholic Christians and allowed them to practice their faith in order to obtain military knowledge and weapons. This aroused the envy and anger of rival *daimyo* who used Buddhism and Shinto to counter the Christian *daimyo*.

Hideyoshi initially favored Christians. However, rivalry between the Christian groups themselves and the arrival of Protestant Dutch traders changed this situation. In 1587, Hideyoshi realized the extent of the Christian influence in Kyushu. He, therefore, abruptly ordered missionaries to leave the country. His edict was not obeyed or enforced, but it marked the end of the favorable reception. Hideyoshi began to unite the *daimyo*. After his death, Ieyasu Tokugawa gained control of the united *daimyo* by becoming the first Shogun in 1603.

The persecution of Christians was based on social and political factors rather than purely religious factors. The exclusive claim of Christianity to be the only true faith and its inability to incorporate other religions, aroused resentment in some circles. Missionaries were regarded as being a potential fifth column preparing the way for Portuguese and Spanish colonialism. The Tokugawa Shogunate chose isolation from the foreign world and was on the alert for any coalition of disaffected elements that might threaten its sovereignty. Christianity was soon viewed as a major threat. Consequently, the persecution became serious and thousands were martyred. The Church began to go underground.

Most missionaries were deported, while others were killed, so that many newly converted Japanese Christians were left without spiritual leadership. On January 27, 1614, Ieyasu Tokugawa's son, Hidetada, issued another edict banning Christianity. This edict demanded the immediate deportation of all foreign missionaries and the local *daimyo* were instructed to destroy Christian churches and to force Japanese Christians to return to the national religions (Harrington, 1993). In addition, rewards in silver were offered to anyone who betrayed Christians by reporting them to government officials. Betrayal of a priest was rewarded with 200 to 500 pieces of silver, reporting a brother with 100 pieces of silver, and reporting a *dojuku* with 50 pieces of silver. This made things hard for Christians. They began to hide, giving rise to a fascinating phenomenon in Christian history: *kakure* (hidden) Christians. In various parts of Japan, there were Christian communities and even villages that maintained their Christian faith for almost 250 years and were not discovered by the authorities until the Meiji period. These hidden Christians were isolated from the Christian world for almost 250 years and they developed their own ways and manners, ceremonies, and religious practices. This has fascinated many scholars and historians both in Japan and overseas.

Organized Persecution

Returning to the persecution, the Tokugawa regime hardened its policy toward Christians. In 1640, a special office called *Kirishitan Shumon Aratame Yaku*, meaning Christian Suppression Office, was established to systematically persecute Christians. The Christian Suppression Office adopted four main tactics to uncover hidden Christians.

The first was the above-mentioned reward system. The second tactic was to force all Japanese residents to become official Buddhists by registering their names at the local or regional Buddhist temple. Failure to register would result in punishment and even the death penalty. The third tactic was the so-called the *gonin gumi seido*. A *gumi* consisted of five or more households who kept order on a local level. These *gumi* were obligated to report any hidden Christians to the authorities. Failure to do so would result in all members of the *gumi* being severely punished together with the Christians. The last tactic was a ceremony known as *fumi-e* or 'picture trampling ceremony'. Everyone was required to trample on a sacred Christian image such as a cross, the Virgin Mary, or Jesus Christ. Later on, for economic reasons, paper images were replaced with metal medals, which lasted longer. These ceremonies were held to detect Christians. Japanese trampled on images of Christ in the streets and alleys of every city, town, and village. Many died because they refused to do so and chose to die as martyrs.

Martyrs of Japan

Japanese soil has witnessed the bloodshed of thousands of Christians, especially during the Tokugawa period. February 5, 1997 was the 400th anniversary of the Christian Holocaust in Japan in which indigenous Japanese Christians were slaughtered for their faith during the 250 years of the Tokugawa period. It all began on February 5, 1597. On the hills of Nagasaki, the blood of 26 martyrs was shed for Christ. These 26 individuals, ranging in age from 12 to 64 years old, were stretched out and crucified on crudely constructed crosses. This slaughter marked the beginning of a nearly 250-year nightmare that decimated the Christian church in Japan. According to Dr. R. Drummond in *A History of the Christian Church in Japan* it was "the largest single organized religious community within the nation" at that time. Today, only about three Japanese in a thousand claim to be Christians.

Five children ranging in age from 12 to 19 were among those killed on February 5. Ibaragi Kun from Kyoto, the youngest of the group being 12 years old, is admired for his remarkable courage in the face of death. Shortly after the Christians had been led to the place of their execution, an official approached him and begged him to recant his faith. Young Ibaragi Kun looked his tormentor squarely in the eye and replied, "Sir, it would be better if you yourself became a Christian and could go to heaven where I am going. Sir, which is my cross?" The stunned official pointed to the smallest of the crosses on the hill. Ibaragi Kun ran forward, knelt in front of it, and embraced it like a friend. Along with the others, he sang praises until he could sing no more.[3]

Christianity During Meiji Period

During the Meiji period, Japan opened her borders to the outside world and many things began to change. The situation regarding Christians also began to change. It was during this period (especially after the introduction of new religious laws in 1873) that Christianity became officially tolerated in Japan.

It was also during the Meiji period that Protestant Christianity was introduced to Japan. Meiji Protestantism was a result of the Meiji Restoration of the late 19th century (see Chapter 2). Japanese Protestantism developed amid transformation, political turmoil, and important policy changes. Politically, Christianity was still considered a foreign faith and it was strongly associated with colonizing Western nations. Thus, Japanese authorities were cautious in their dealings with Christians. Despite this, Protestant missionaries first arrived in Japan in 1859. However, missionaries were initially restricted to a few large cities and Japanese were still prohibited from becoming Christians (Lande, 1989).

Protestantism was transmitted to Japan through two channels. The first was through church agencies and mission boards sending missionaries. The first missionaries that came via this channel arrived in Japan in 1859. They represented Western missionary movements. They were not invited; rather, they came to Japan on their own initiative. In contrast, in the other channel, Protestants were invited or offered employment by Japanese agencies. One of the first Protestant missionaries in Japan, Reverend G. F. Verbeck, was employed by the Japanese government for a considerable time. He functioned as an advisor in various capacities. Several Protestants who arrived in Japan as government-employed instructors exerted a profound influence on Protestant history (ibid).

Converts

Converts in the Meiji period can be classified into two groups: samurai converts and converts from the farming class. The majority of early Protestant converts were from the samurai class. The samurai class was more open to Christianity since their children attended Western schools and they had more contact with Westerners than other Japanese people. They had also had access to Chinese Bibles and some had already read it.

Like the samurai, farmers were hungry for modern knowledge and they adopted new lifestyles suited for the demands of the changing world. Converts found in Christianity a new socio-ethical concept that emphasized the equality of all humanity since Christianity taught that all were created by God and could be redeemed by Christ. This concept was readily accepted by those who had been considered inferior to the warrior class in the feudal age (ibid). Finally, converts saw Christianity as the fulfillment of Confucianism. Many of these converts were zealous for their faith. Verbeck writes, "After a week or two the Japanese, for the first time in the history of their nation, were on their knees in a Christian prayer meeting, entreating God with great emotion, with tears streaming down their faces, that he would give his Spirit to Japan as to the early church and to the people around the apostles . . . As a direct fruit of these prayer meetings, the first Christian church was organized in Yokohama on March 10, 1872 (Lande, 1989).

Modernization and Christianity

The question arose: which path should Japan take in her modernization? The majority believed in Western technology, but a minority believed that Japan should be modernized through the Christian faith. Some Japanese intellectuals strongly promoted Christianity and adapted it to the Japanese situation. One of these men was J. H. Neesima. He was from the samurai class and had an outstanding personality. He converted to Christianity and then studied theology in the US. His dream was to modernize Japan through the Christian faith. On returning to Japan, he founded the Doshisha School, which later became a well-regarded university.

Christians in Japan directly or indirectly supported the modernization of Japan in various areas, especially education. Either missionaries were invited to Japan or they came of their own accord to educate the young in languages and sciences. These teachers had the opportunity to share their faith with the Japanese. Many schools exerted a significant influence on society.

Christian women also exerted an increasing influence on society.

Many women's groups, large and small, national and local, Christian and non-Christian, were active in society. The most active members were Christian women, or at least those who were sympathetic to Christianity, because until quite recently women had received higher education only from Christian missionaries. The sympathy to Christians gradually began to wane and they came under strong pressure. The refusal of Uchimura Kanzo to bow down to the Imperial Seal in the presence of a 1000 students and 60 teachers, caused great humiliation since the authorities considered the Emperor to be a god. Tensions began to grow and some Christian were closed down.

Catholicism during the Meiji period

Catholics mainly focused the efforts on regaining the 250 years old hidden church, the hidden Christians. Some converted back to Catholicism, but many continued to practice their own way of worship. It was too hard for them to suddenly change their Christian rites to Catholic ones. Therefore, the Catholics referred to those hidden Christians as "the separated ones!"

CHRISTIANITY

IN **JAPAN**

PART **FOUR**

Chapter Nine

Christianity
in Contemporary Japan

Christianity has not flourished in Japan as it has in some of Japan's Asian neighbors, particularly China, South Korea, and the Philippines. Christianity is still considered a foreign faith that is not suitable for ordinary Japanese.

Practicing Christianity in Japan has not always been easy and sometimes it can be quite frustrating. Many Japanese feel that if they become a Christian they will relinquish some of their 'Japaneseness.' Becoming a Christian is often viewed as betraying Japanese culture. Christians are frequently perceived as being antisocial and selfish for disrupting the harmony of the family unit by refusing to observe many traditional Shinto and Buddhist rituals, especially those of praying to spirits and reverencing the dead. Many associate the Christian faith with the West and thus consider it to be incompatible with Japanese culture. While they tolerate the Christian church, many Japanese feel that the Christian faith does not really belong in Japan. Currently, a mere 0.22% of Japan's population attends Christian services. Such figures raise serious concerns about the future of the Christian church in Japan. Some predict that in 20 years' time nearly 50% of churches will be vacant since Japan's elderly church members will have passed away and no young people will replenish the churches.

Furthermore, attracting new members is like trying "to draw water with a bamboo basket" (an ancient Japanese proverb). The future is now as far as the 9,000-member Reformed Church in Japan is concerned. If this 53-year old denomination is to survive, it must instill the gospel in its young members whose leadership can form the foundation of Japan's reformed faith. It must overcome its weaknesses and go forward into the new century (Moni, 2004).

General Information

With less than 1.5% practicing Christians, Japan is considered one of the most unreached people groups in the world. Catholics, Protestants, Independents, Anglicans, Orthodox, Evangelicals, Charismatics, and Pentecostals are some of the many Christian groups that can be found in Japan today.

According to Operation World (Mandryk, 2010), the annual growth rate of Christianity in Japan is –0.2%. This is lower than the annual growth rate of 0.1% reported in the 2001 edition of Operation World. Thus, Christianity is currently experiencing negative growth. In 2001, Pentecostalism, with 3.4%, was the fastest growing church in Japan (Johnstone and Mandryk, 2001). However, this decreased to 1.1% in 2010 (Mandryk, 2010). Anglicans had an annual growth rate of 1.6% in 2001 and are now experiencing a growth rate of 0%. Evangelicalism is also declining at a rate of -0.4% per year (ibid). Orthodox Christianity currently has the highest annual growth rate of any Christian denomination of 1.5%.

In 2001, Islam had an annual growth rate of 6.1% a year, making it the fastest growing faith in Japan. This growth rate was due to immigrants coming to Japan for work rather than conversions. However, the annual growth rate of Islam in Japan decreased to 1.3% in 2010 due to restricted immigration policies.

Despite such statistics, a recent poll conducted by the Gallup Research Group indicates that 6% of Japanese claim to be Christian. The Gallup researchers were surprised by the high numbers of teenagers who claimed to be Christians (Christian Examiner Online, 2006) (some claim that George Gallup corrected this percentage from 6% to 4%; even though this correction is not easily verifiable, I think it is important to mention it here). It is appropriate to mention here, that unlike Operation World, the Gallup report is only a poll and it does not reflect per se the overall picture of the Christianity in Japan.

View of Christianity

As mentioned above, many Japanese people consider Christianity to be a foreign religion. Because of the historical and political background, the Christian faith is associated with bitter occurrences of the past such as colonialism and the hidden agenda of the West to infiltrate Japan. Furthermore, the atomic attacks on Hiroshima and Nagasaki by the US, a Western superpower, reinforced antipathy toward Christianity. This disinterest combined with sometimes ineffective evangelism has resulted in non-Japanese being unaware of how the Japanese people view Christianity.

Japanese people borrow certain aspects of Christianity. For example, at Christmas, Japanese people decorate Christmas trees and buy presents for each other. Also, many modern Japanese weddings are 'Christian' weddings in which the couple gets married in a 'church', the bride wears a white wedding dress, and the bridegroom wears a suit. However, while all these customs come from Western culture, they are not elements of the true Christian faith. The Japanese people have borrowed these cultural elements, but not the real message and essence of the gospel of Jesus Christ.

In addition to this, the Japanese church is demographically aging. Leadership positions in churches are dominated by old people, many of whom find it difficult to relate to young people and cope with recent high-tech developments. The average age of pastors in Japan is approaching 60 and 75% of pastors are over 55. There are more Japanese pastors over 80 than there are under 30.[1]

Korean immigrants have been very active in church planting and evangelizing the Japanese. However, the racial issues described above make it difficult for them to attract more Japanese to the Christian faith. One thing I have personally noticed when I travel in Japan is that there are growing international churches, some led by Japanese and some by immigrant pastors from Asia and Africa. These churches are mixtures of Filipinos, Africans, other Asians, and even

Europeans. Could these immigrants play a major role in shaping the future of Christianity in Japan?

Some Barriers

One of the greatest challenges that Christians face is that of seeking to proclaim Jesus Christ as the one true and living God. Many Japanese would happily embrace Jesus as another great teacher. However, they consider the claim of Christ's deity to be arrogant and offensive.

The second challenge is the Japanese concept of religion. As mentioned above, Japanese people believe that there are many *kami* or gods. These gods do not have any concept of evil or good, right and wrong. In contrast, Christianity is a faith of right and wrong, good and evil. This makes it difficult for the Japanese to believe in only one God.

Thirdly, during the Allied occupation of Japan, the Allied forces (including Americans) forced the Japanese Emperor to deny his deity as part of the democratization process. The Japanese people considered their Emperor to be a god (*a kami*), a direct descendant of the sun goddess, Amaterasu Omikami. Many older Japanese people may still resent the fact that Western nations and so-called 'Christian' nations forced the emperor to deny his deity.

Finally, the working lifestyle of Japan and the pressure for Christians to attend Sunday services are incompatible. The long working hours and the lack of family time make it difficult for Japanese Christians to go to church on Sundays.

Chapter Ten

Japanese Theology

In his book, *Japanese Contribution to Christian Theology* (1960), Carl Michelson indicates that even though Protestant Christianity is relatively young in Japan, Japan is apparently the first country to develop its own significant theology (Michelson, 1960). Since Meiji Japan, the Japanese Christian scholars have been attempting to bridge the gap between Christianity and Japanese native religions and culture by creating a Japanese. These attempts at contextualization have often been criticized by Western missionaries or by Japanese theologians who were strongly influenced by Western theology. The arrival of American missionaries after Word War II, in response to the request by General MacArthur was a mixed blessing for the devastated post-war country: the missionaries brought humanitarian aid, education, and the gospel but they delayed the indigenization of Christianity to the late 1960s.

Early Cultural Theological Tensions

Japanese people struggle with various issues that Western Christianity is often unable to address adequately. One problematic area is the question of what happened to Japanese people who died before they had the chance to hear the gospel. This question is asked by almost every Japanese who is evangelized by Western missionaries. Of course, missionaries try to answer this question as sensitively as possible, but ultimately they will mention hell. A Japanese woman once told a missionary trying to evangelize her that she would rather spend eternity in hell with her ancestors than in the paradise preached by Christians. If the Christian God has no solution to the fact that her ancestors did not have a chance to hear about Jesus, she would rather spend all eternity in hell. Some theologians have tried to explain the concept of hell in a Japanese context, but they have often been misunderstood by other Christians.

Another aspect of Christianity that Japanese struggle with is the claim that the Bible is the infallible word of God. For instance, Kozaki Hiromichi (1856–1928), a Japanese theologian, believed that the theory of evolution and the Bible could be harmonized and this influenced his understanding of the Bible. For Kozaki, faith and reason are not in conflict with each other, but are rather mutually interdependent, which results in what he called *reason sanctified by the Holy Spirit*. This caused him to suggest that the Bible is inspired by God, but this does not mean that its words are literally infallible (Furuya, 1997). This view was criticized by Western missionaries and some Japanese theologians such as Uemura Masahisa (1861–1925), whose theology was strongly influenced by Western theology.

Another aspect that Japanese have found difficult to accept is the lack of bridges between Christianity and the other main religions of Japan, Buddhism and Shintoism (and Confucianism). In the early Protestant period in Japan, theologians tried to create a dialogue, but they were either misunderstood or they went too far in their interpretations. Ebina Danjo (1886–1937) tried to combine Confucianism and Shintoism with Christianity. According to him, Christianity was a universal truth that was valid for Japanese practicing a Confucian way of life and for those who pursue Shintoism. He believed that when Shintoism is purified, it becomes Christianity. Throughout his life, he was constantly criticized for his views. Yet, according to him, he remained a follower of Christ until the end of his life.

Furthermore, independent Japanese churches, especially pre-war churches, have a negative attitude toward denominational differences. Even today, they are skeptical about denominational and doctrinal differences. For instance, Uchimura Kanzo (1861–1930) who started the non-Church (mukyokai) movement. *Mukyokai* is a Christianized version of *mushukyo* (non-religious). Uchimura believed that non-church is the true form of the church. He rejected the idea of an organized church and believed that there is no organized church in heaven, citing Revelation 21:22. He believed that bishops, deacons, preachers, and teachers exist only here on earth. He thought that there would be neither baptism nor communion, neither teachers nor students in heaven. In 1926, he wrote:

> *I am blamed by the missionaries for upholding Japanese Christianity. They say that Christianity is a universal religion, and to uphold Japanese Christianity is to make a universal religion a national religion. Very true! But do not these very missionaries uphold sectional or denominational forms of Christianity which are not very different from national Christianity? Is not Episcopalianism essentially an English Christianity, Presbyterianism a Scotch Christianity, Lutheranism a German Christianity, and so forth? Why, for instance, call a universal religion "Cumberland Presbyterianism?" If it is not wrong to apply the name of a district in the state of Kentucky to Christianity, why is it wrong to apply the name of my country to the same? I think I have as much right to call my Christianity Japanese as thousands of Christians in Cumberland Valley have the right to call their Christianity by the name of the valley they live in (Mullins, 1998).*

Theological studies flourished in pre-war Japan. Uemura Masahisa (1861–1925) promoted Evangelical theology with an American flavor. He also founded Tokyo Theological Seminary (now Tokyo Union Theological Seminary). Uemura strongly opposed Ebina's theology. Japan has many great theologians, including Sato Shigehiko (1887–1935), Yamaya Seigo (1889–1982), Otsuka Setsuji (1887–1977), Takakura Tokutaro (1885–1934), and many others; the majority of them were mentored by Uemura. For instance, Takakura Tokukaro's book, *Evangelical Christianity,* published in 1924, became a bestseller. Takakura was a disciple of Uemura and continued his mentor's legacy and theological views. Takakura introduced Evangelicalism with a German flavor, and is known as the man who introduced Calvinism to Japan. During the 1920s, German theologies became influential in Japan. Sato Shigehiko introduced Luther to

Japanese Christians. Takakura believed that Catholicism, Liberalism, and cultural Christianity are influenced by pagan elements and thus do not represent pure Christianity. He opposed liberalism and humanism that he saw "sneaking" into the Christian message.

During the Meiji period, Social Christianity, a combination of socialism and the Christian message, became popular among some Japanese theologians. Kagawa Toyohiko (1888–1960) is a well-known figure in this movement. He is known for his labor movement activities in Japan and was supported by Christian students. Leaders such as Nakajima Shigeru (1888–1946), Kimura Yonetaru (1889–1949), and Kan Enkichi (1895–1972) influenced the Social Christianity movement. Nakajima Shigeru founded the National Alliance for Social Christianity in 1933. Nakajima emphasized the difference between community and associations/organizations. Churches and labor unions are examples of associations since they have sets of rules and regulations. Associations are based on sets of rules, but communities are based on personal relationships and only love causes the community to grow. The emphasis was on doing good and helping the poor and the suffering. Despite being called Social Christianity, the movement strongly opposed Marxism. It had its own unique ideologies, with Christ as an abstract concept for the concrete process of socialization, which Nakajima called redemptive love. He believed that a society where selfless love is practiced is close to the Kingdom of God. The process by which a society grows toward such selfless love is called socialization. Since the concept of "Christ" for him is the same as socialization and since Jesus is the only person who fully manifested this "socialization", he redeems us from sin. The root of sin is selfish and egoistic social motivations, and salvation can only be realized through Jesus Christ and following his example of selfless love.

Japanese Christianity was also influenced by Karl Barth's theology, known as Dialectical Theology: God can only reveal Himself vertically from heaven to his children. Of course, Jesus Christ is the center of such revelations and the Bible is the place where we come to know God. Theologians like Kumano Yoshitaka promoted this theology among the Japanese. Barth's theology was welcomed in Japan because the Japanese saw a degree of intellectualism in Barth's theology. Japanese Christians have often desired a theology that is simultaneously intellectual and inspirational.

There are many other pre-war theologians whose names deserve to be mentioned here. However, I wish to discuss some Japanese theologians who were active in the post-war period and developed significant theological ideas that influenced Christianity in Japan. Post-war Japan produced great theologians such as Kitamori Kazoh (1916–1998) who introduced the theology of the pain of God. He believed that the essence of the gospel lay in the redemptive pain and suffering of God and that human pain is symbolic of God's pain. Kitamori compared the pain of God with the concept of *tsurasa* that appears in Japanese literature. *Tsurasa* means to suffer in order to save others from pain. In Kitamori's eyes, God the Father suffered by sacrificing His Son in order to redeem humanity. This is *tsurasa* love: enduring pain for the sake of another. Yagi Seiichi was another theologian who promoted intercultural and inter-theological dialogue with Buddhism. Yagi looked for similarities between Christianity and Buddhism.

Theological differences were not the only causes of disputes between foreign missionaries and Japanese believers. The ethnocentric arrogance of missionaries made Western Christianity unbearable to many Japanese believers. Matsumura Kaiseki (1859–1939), an early convert of the Dutch Reformed missionary James Ballagh and a member of the Yokohama Band, illustrates the tensions that existed between missionaries and their students. Matsumura, who had returned to Ballagh's school to assist with teaching and supervising students, recalls that on one occasion he explained to Ballagh that their missionary work would be of no avail if they continued to treat the Japanese as no more than cooks or helpers. In response, Mr. Ballagh's wife accused Matsumura of being possessed by the devil because of the things he said (Mullins, 1998). He was dismissed from his position at the school and was isolated from the missionaries. Soon Matsumura started his own independent denomination, called

The Way. Joseph Kitagawa explains:

> *"More often than not, European and American missionaries attempted to Westernize as well as Christianize the Japanese people and culture. Japanese converts were made to feel, consciously or unconsciously, that to decide for Christ also implied the total surrender of their souls to the missionaries. The task of evangelism was interpreted by most missionaries as transplanting the Western church onto Japanese soil, including the ugly features of denominationalism—an unhappy assumption, indeed" (ibid).*

Indigenous Christianity

From about the second half of the 20th century onwards, Japanese Christians sought to develop a Japanese Christianity that was not based only on German or American doctrines. I personally believe that this attempt was a revival of the earlier movement in the mid-Meiji period, which had slowed due to Japan's involvement in the war, the surrender of Japan, and the entry of thousands of American and Western missionaries after the war. I believe Japanese Christians have often hoped for an indigenous version of Christianity but did not fully get the chance to create it. After the war and the rebuilding of Japan, the time was ripe for such indigenization.

According to Takeda Kiyedo, indigenization can be classified into five main types: (1) the buried type in which religion is buried and lost through compromise; (2) the isolation type, which isolates and refuses to compromise; (3) the confrontation type; (4) the grafting type in which fusion keeps confrontation in the background; and (5) the apostasy type, which paradoxically seeks indigenization through apostasy (Odagaki, 1997). Takeda herself preferred a grafting approach in which Christianity confronts indigenous Japanese culture by burying itself in and becoming fused with Japanese soil while at the same time maintaining a posture of confrontation as suggested by the parable of the grain of wheat (ibid).

Various theologians before and after the war promoted an indigenized form of Christianity. They argued that if Jewish Christians used Jewish texts as their canon, why could Japanese Christians draw on Buddhist and Shinto literature? Some believed that these sacred books (e.g., the Buddhist scriptures and Shinto texts) referred to Christ and foreshadowed His coming—that Christ was the fulfillment of these sacred and ancient Japanese scriptures. Of course, not all of the indigenous movements believed this. Most indigenous theologians, including Uchimura Kanzo, believed in the canonical books of Scripture. The indigenous movements included the Non-church Movement founded by Uchimura in 1901; the Way, founded by Matsumura Kaiseki in 1907, Christ Heart Church, founded by Kawai Shinsui in 1927; Japan Ecclesia of Christ, founded by Koike Tatsuo in 1940; the Original Gospel Tabernacle, founded by Teshima Ikuro in 1948; and Okinawa Christian Gospel, founded by Nakahara in 1977. Many other movements deserve mention but cannot be discussed here due to space limitations. This list is only an indication of the many communities that were established as a reaction to the problematic strategies of foreign missionaries.

Chapter Eleven

Christianity's Contribution to Japanese Life

According to Reischauer "the influence of Christianity on modern Japanese society is far greater than the small number of its adherents would suggest. Christians are strongly represented among the best-educated, leading elements in society and have therefore exerted a quite disproportionate influence" (Reischauer, 1998). In this chapter, I therefore discuss this latter point from several perspectives, by giving a general overview that is not limited to any particular period in Japanese history. The contributions of Christianity fall into the following major categories: education, social justice, and intellectual life.

Contributions in the Field of Education

Thanks to the efforts of missionaries, various schools and universities were established to advance the Christian faith in Japan and, at the same time, to teach science, technology, and foreign languages. During the Meiji Period, the cause of Christian education was strengthened by the opening of institutions such as Aoyama University, Meiji University, and Toyo Eiwa University (Clement, 1905). People like Neesima Joseph (1843–1890) were able to interest not only Christians, but also non-Christians in working to establish Doshisha University. Further, Christianity helped to established girl's schools in Japan (Nishiyama, 1911). Some of Japan's well-known women's colleges have Christian roots. For example, Tokyo Woman's Christian University was found by Nitobe Inazo (1863–1933), and Tsuda College, a private women's college was found by Tsuda Umeko (1864–1929) (Hastings, 2007). Throughout the Tokugawa Period, such schools were a rarity — the natural result of the nationally held conviction that education for women was unnecessary and of little value.

During the Meiji Period and later, Christian missionaries observed that there were few opportunities for Japanese women to obtain an education. The national neglect of their education became clear to them and they responded by establishing schools for girls. Their efforts resulted in the building of several schools in different parts of Japan. The girls who have been educated in these Christian schools have demonstrated the good results that women's education can produce (ibid).

In 1890, the number of public high schools for girls increased. Government reports in 1903 state that the number of schools for girls had increased to 155 by that point, and that the total number of students enrolled in them was 35,546. All of them were under the direction of 1,094 women teachers (ibid). It should never be forgotten that by word and deed, by work and inspiration, the Christian mission provided a strong impetus for the recognition and solution of this problem in Japan. They made it clear that such education was vitally necessary (ibid).

According Nishiyama, the good results obtained from educating Japanese girls through the enthusiastic efforts of Christian missionaries brought about two important changes in Japanese society: they produced an unvarying belief in the need for women's education, and they improved woman's position in Japanese society (Nishiyama, 1911). Those Japanese girls who received an education showed that Japanese women had an undreamed of capacity for companionship and efficiency. Nishiyama argues that the Japanese should therefore fully appreciate the debt Japanese civilization owes to Christian missionaries in the education of girls (ibid). Thanks to their past efforts, a large number of Japanese women are now able to receive an education in various fields. Some Japanese women have entered the business world. Women graduates of the Christian girls' schools were infused with new values of human worth, introduced to a new vision of womanhood. Although the primary goal of the

Christian girls' education was evangelistic, with the passage of time these schools developed into excellent academic institutions offering sophisticated curricula. This eventually produced prestigious seats of higher learning in modern Japan (Li, 1993).

Contributions to Social Justice

Japanese Christians also became important pioneers and leaders in the fields of social justice and social welfare. Prominent personalities included Kanzo Uchimura, who criticized Japan's occupation of Korea (Howes, 2005), and the social and labor rights activist and author, Kagawa Toyohiko (1888–1960).

The Christian contribution to the improvement of social welfare in Japan is widely recognized. Early efforts at social reform, extending medical care to all, and social work were considered to be a natural part of the Roman Catholic and Protestant mission to the country (Endo, 2003).

Women's Rights

Although the Meiji restoration offered Japanese women a chance to make a new start, it did not actually improve their social position much. They were merely incorporated into the industrialization and modernization processes and used as a source of cheap labor. The transformation from a feudal society into an industrial capitalist one resulted in various changes in attitude and this, in turn, led to riots and strikes. Moreover, these changes in attitude eventually influenced the social position of women and led to the development of various women's movements in Japan. They began as a strong protest against the miserable position of women during the Meiji era.

The very first women's movements in Japan were influenced by Christianity, and they sought to abolish legal prostitution in Japan. The *Women's Temperance Association* in Japan was the counterpart of various Western organizations such as the Women's Christian Temperance Union. One well-known movement in Japan, *Jiyu Minken Undo* or Movement for Freedom and Popular Rights began in the

1880s. Kishida Toshiko (1864–1901) and Fukuda Hideko (1865–1927) were the central figures in this (Hastings, 2007). Kishida's strong and charismatic speeches inspired many Japanese women. She fought for equal rights on their behalf. Fukuda later joined Kishida and together they began the Popular Rights Movement. As mentioned earlier, another example of a prominent Christian woman in Japan is Tsuda Umeko (1864–1929), a feminist, educator, and pioneer in education for women during the Meiji Period (ibid). Many other movements and various famous personalities, including Yosano Akiko (1878–1942), Hiratsuka Raicho (1886– 1971), and socialist Hiratsuka Kikue (1890–1980), promoted the feminist movement in Japan (ibid).

Societal Minorities

Missionaries and native Christians have also played significant role in Japanese society by supporting minorities and the poor. During the Meiji Period, many *burakumin* embraced Christianity. Christian churches and missionaries offered support to them and other minorities. Yamagami Takujyu was one of the pioneers of the Catholic movement for the liberation of the *buraku* people. Born in 1855, he himself was a *buraku* who became a Christian and decided to fight for the rights of his people. The Catholic Church even has a special commission for this, namely, the Japan Catholic Committee for *Buraku* issues.[1]

One of the well-known Christian activists who helped the poor and vulnerable was Kagawa Toyohiko (1888–1960). Kagawa is also known as the "Saint Francis of Japan" (Mullins, 2007). He lived long enough throughout pre- and post-World War II to prove himself to be one of most influential Christian figures on the social justice scene in Japan. In 1909, Kagawa moved into a Kobe slum as a Japanese missionary and social worker. His aim was to help the poverty stricken people of

---

1 - "From the booklet "The History of Buraku Discrimination and the Catholic Church in Japan" at the 4th Symposium on the Bible and Discrimination was held at Kawara-Machi Church in Kyoto in September 1995. (Kyoto: Japan Catholic Committee for Buraku Issues).

that area. Based on his experience there, he published *Researches in the Psychology of the Poor* (1916). In 1921 and 1922 he was arrested for his part in labor activism during strikes. While in prison he wrote the novels *Crossing the Deathline* and *Shooting at the Sun*. The former was a semi-autobiographical depiction of his time among Kobe's destitute. Kagawa organized the Japanese Federation of Labor as well as the National Anti-War League in 1928. He continued to evangelize Japan's poor, to advocate for women's suffrage and call for a peaceful foreign policy. In 1954 and 1955, Kagawa was nominated for the Nobel Peace Prize. He was posthumously awarded the country's second-highest honor, namely, induction in the *Order of the Sacred Treasure*.

Relief Work

When it comes to Christian relief work, one must certainly also mention the support extended to the Japanese society by of thousands of missionaries and native Christians. For example *Operation Japan*[2] writes the following about the homeless people in Sanya and the role of Christian churches there:

> *The number of homeless in the nation reached 20,000 by the end of 1999, up 26% from six months previous. About 84% of that number are concentrated in Tokyo's 23 wards and the cities of Yokohama, Kawasaki, Nagoya and Osaka. Most conspicuous in increases were Tokyo's 23 wards, where the homeless population increased from 4,300 to 5,800, up 35%. One of the most concentrated areas is the Taito Ward, slum area of Sanya. The Salvation Army and several churches are seeking to minister to these people. Most visible among those ministering is the Seikawa (Holy River) Christian Evangelical Church in Sanya, under the leadership of Pastor Haruko Morimoto. She has*

---

2 - Operation Japan (OJ) is a resource available on CD-ROM. It was developed by *Reaching Japanese For Christ*. OJ contains relevant information about Christianity by prefecture in Japan. More information can be found at the website (http://www.rjcnetwork.org).

ministered in that area for 29 years, has served over 1.2 million meals, and baptized nearly 3,000 people. The Sanya Church completed a new large chapel in 1998 which includes lodging facilities for some of the homeless. Pastor Morimoto has become well known throughout Japan for her unique ministry of love and confrontation. Her loud shouts of "Hallelujah!" continue to encourage many who have little hope for rescue (ibid).

Both in the past, during the post-World War II era, and in the present after the recent earthquake and tsunami of March 2011, Christians, both individuals and organizations, have been visibly active. Christian relief services provide medical care, shelter, food supplies and moral support.

Over the years, The Japan Evangelical Association's (JEA) Relief and Development Commission has been active in calamity-stricken areas and so provided a good testimony for the evangelical churches. CRASH Japan (Christian Relief, Assistance, Support, and Hope) is a non-profit Christian disaster relief organization based in Tokyo; it is officially recognized by the Japanese government. Before a disaster strikes, they equip and prepare churches and missions so that they can respond effectively. When disaster does strike, CRASH mobilizes Christian volunteers to work with churches and other local ministries. The organization Samaritan's Purse, along with other relief ministries like CRASH and World Vision, has done an outstanding job with its ministry in Japan. The disaster relief in Tohoku after the earthquake and tsunami on March 11 is a case in point (ibid).

Contributions to Various Areas of Intellectual Life

Literature plays a significant role in Japanese culture and society. Japanese people enjoy reading novels. Some Christians are numbered among Japan's most prominent novelists. According to Takado Kaname, by the end of 1945, there was not a single active Christian writer in Japan, but by 1970 there were over 20 (Tadako, 1991). In Takado's assessment, Japanese Christian novelists not only struggle to be Christian, and remain so, in a society in which Christians are in the minority, but they also struggle to both be Japanese and preserve their reputation as authors (ibid). Takado compares the Japanese Christian writers of post-World War II to a voice crying in the wilderness imbued with the hope of resurrection, freedom from the annihilating force of death (ibid). Takado praises the significance of the country's Christian writers' overall contribution to Japanese society. Presently, the Japanese population, both Christian and non-Christian, reads the works of Japanese Christian authors. Their literary works transcend ideological and theological conflicts, overcome denominational barriers, and diminish perceived differences between Christian and non-Christian. For this reason they also provide an open forum for reading and dialogue (ibid). One of the main contributions of Japanese Christian authors is that they have produced a wealth of literature that articulates the Christian faith and thought in the indigenous idiom of the Japanese people and their daily life (ibid).

Endo Shusaku (1923-1996) is one of the most well-known of Japanese writers in the West. At least seven of his novels are now available in translation. He is unusual among Japanese writers because of his frequent treatment of Christian themes (Napier, 1996). His works are often historical in nature, such as *Chinmoku* (1966) (trans. *Silence* (1961)) and *Samurai* (1980) (trans. *The Samurai* (1982)). According to Napier, many of them deal with the miraculous within the framework of questions of faith. *Sukyandaru* (1986) (trans. *Scandal* (1988)) is perhaps the most explicitly 'fantastic' of all his writings (ibid).

Endo, however, is not the only Christian writer in Japan. The appendix includes a list of Japanese Christian novelists. Among them are Shiina Rinzo (1911–1973), Ishihara Yoshiro (1915–1977), Mori Arimasa (1912–1976), Fukunaga Takehiko (1918–1979), Shimao Toshio (1917–1986), Ariyoshi Sawako (1913–1984), Ogawa Kunio (1927–2008), Sono Ayako (1931–), Miura Shumon (1926–), Sakato Hiro (1924–), Ohara Tomie (1912–2000), Takahashi Takako (1932–), Moriuchi Toshio (1936–), Kaga Otohiko (1929–), Tanaka Komimasa (1925–2000) and Miura Ayako (1922–1999). Almost every author on the list has won various prestigious awards for their work. Fujimura Makoto is a well-known contemporary Christian artist, who is recognized worldwide as a cultural shaper. A presidential appointee to the National Council on the Arts from 2003-2009, Fujimura served as an international advocate for the arts, speaking with decision makers and advising governmental policies on the arts.[3] Fujimura's work is exhibited at galleries around the world, including Dillon Gallery in New York, Sato Museum in Tokyo, The Contemporary Museum of Tokyo, Tokyo National University of Fine Arts Museum, Bentley Gallery in Arizona, Gallery Exit and Oxford House at Taikoo Place in Hong Kong, and Vienna's Belvedere Museum (ibid).

Even though this chapter was not intended to be an extended report on the contribution of Christianity to the Japanese society and culture, it does, I believe, nevertheless make it clear that Christianity has indeed influenced Japan, specifically that it has contributed to the social and cultural development of this nation. It might not have acquired vast numbers of adherents, but its influence runs deeper than it may initially seem.

---

3 - www.makotofujimura.com/bio

JAPANESE
CULTURE & **CHRISTIAN** FAITH

PART **FIVE**

Chapter 12

Elements of Japanese Culture

Before we can understand the Japanese, we need to have some idea of what their daily lives are like, including their traditions, beliefs, and worldviews. Many books, articles, and documentaries have been produced on Japanese culture. Japanese culture seems to hold a fascination for thousands of scholars and researchers all around the world.

Japanese culture is said to be unique and to contain elements not found anywhere else. I personally doubt this. I believe that the elements that seem unique to Japan can be found in other cultures. For example, there are many similarities between some elements of Japanese and Iranian cultures. Consider, for instance, the concept of *aimai*, which means 'ambiguity', 'indirectness', and 'not giving direct answers.' Avoiding saying "No" is considered very Japanese. Japanese people tend to be indirect to show respect and politeness. If someone asks another person whether they would like coffee or tea, they will probably answer 'either is fine'. The same concept is found among Iranians. Iranians can be very indirect in some matters and they use words such as 'perhaps', 'maybe', and 'it does not matter' to be polite and indirect.

It is also said that it is difficult to know what a Japanese person really thinks. What they say may be totally different from what they think. This is also found in Iranian culture. Sometimes Iranians do not say what they really believe and think, but they smile or laugh and just agree or say things that they may disagree with.

I am not suggesting that Iranian culture is identical with Japanese culture, for there are many differences. However, there are also similarities. I believe such similarities may be found among many different cultures; I do not believe in the absolute uniqueness of any culture. However, to a certain degree every culture has its own specific elements.

This chapter discusses some key concepts of Japanese culture and considers cultural values, attitudes, behavior patterns, and communication styles in contemporary Japan. It is not possible to describe all the cultural elements; rather, certain important elements are discussed in this chapter. I systematically refer to the book, *The Japanese Mind: Understanding Contemporary Japanese Culture* edited by Roger J. Davies and Osamu Ikeno, which clearly describes Japanese culture in a simple and understandable way. This chapter also considers how these cultural elements hinder or assist the spread of the Christian message.

Honne / Tatemae

Honne means 'informal, personal reality in disregard of social parameters', while *tatemae* means 'official, public and socially required or politically correct.' *Honne* is an opinion or an action motivated by a person's true inner feelings, whereas *tatemae* is an opinion or action influenced by social norms. Thus, *honne* refers to a person's deep beliefs or intentions, while *tatemae* refers to socially tuned motives or intentions that are shaped, encouraged, or suppressed by majority norms. These two concepts are often considered dichotomous and contrast genuinely held personal feelings and convictions from those that are socially controlled. Another dimension of this dichotomy is that *honne* is expressed privately, while *tatemae* may be openly professed.

During the formalities of a business meeting, a Japanese business man tends to follow protocol. Later, while enjoying conversation with his colleagues over a glass of beer or sake (rice wine), the same person will frankly express his *honne* regarding the issues raised at the meeting. Aiming at peace and harmony, the public self avoids confrontation, whereas the private self tends toward sincere self-expression.

When trying to understand *honne* and *tatemae* and how these contrasting concepts function in Japan, it is important to examine certain cultural characteristics such as the dislike of directly expressing opinions for fear that it might hurt the feelings of others and the importance of harmony and ceremony. Japanese people are usually careful about what they say and they often use *tatemae* in order to get along well with others. For example, when a person is visiting someone's house in Japan and it becomes time for supper, people will often say, "Won't you dine with us?" However, this is not really an invitation; rather it is a subtle hint that it is time to go home. To those from other countries this may sound confusing, but for Japanese it is a natural way to interact socially. So the correct response to, "Won't you dine with us?" is "Thank you very much, but I am not hungry." This type of behavior is formulaic in Japanese society (Davies and Ikeno, 2002).

Honne/tatemae may be a natural part of Japanese society, but it may cause problems. For example, the relationship between a husband and wife may be hindered by it since they do not express their true feelings but merely say what is required from them—a politically correct relationship. In reality, the couple may be suffering inside. Women and children are often victims of this.

Honne/tatemae causes Japanese people to keep their worldview or religious beliefs to themselves so that they do not share them with others. Japanese Christians should be free from this concept. They may consider that their faith to be something personal and that their personal beliefs do not matter when they are with others. They feel pressure to behave in a politically/socially correct manner by going along with the group and society and not sharing the gospel with other people. I believe that *honne/tatemae* is a cultural stronghold of Japan that hinders Japanese Christians from sharing their faith with others.

Uchi / Soto

Japanese culture divides a person's world into two groups: *uchi*, an inner group to which the person belongs, and *soto*, which refers to everyone not in the *uchi* group. The relationship between *uchi* and *soto* is complex since they do not remain static; they may overlap and vary with time as a person's situation changes. *Uchi/soto* groups may be conceptualized as a series of overlapping circles. A person's position within a group and relationship with other groups will depend on the context, situation, and time of life. For example, a person will usually have a family, a job, and other groups or organizations to which they belong. Their position within the various groups and relationship with other groups will vary with the position they have at a given moment. Thus, a company employee may have a high position within the company but have a humble role in relation to the company's customers. The same employee may hold a black belt in karate giving them a superior position within their karate club, but they may be a beginner at tennis and thus occupy an inferior position in the tennis club, and so on.

Uchi and *soto* are associated with clean and unclean. One's house is considered clean, but outside the house is considered unclean and dirty. Children learn to distinguish between *uchi* and *soto* at an early age; for example, a child's house, class, or school is considered as *uchi* depending on the level and situation.

As mentioned earlier, *uchi/soto* operates on various levels. On the highest level, the entire country of Japan could be considered as *uchi* and the outside world as soto. Japanese generally refer to people from other countries as outsiders ("*gaijin*") no matter how long they have lived in Japan or how well they speak Japanese. The Japanese clearly distinguish insiders from outsiders in daily life based on *uchi* or *soto*. This concept of *uchi/soto* has greatly influenced Japanese society, especially in terms of human relations (Davies and Ikeno, 2002).

The *uchi/soto* concept promotes group consciousness. Groups are very important since Japanese society is not an individualistic society and disturbing the group may be considered inappropriate and impolite. For instance, students generally do not ask teachers questions in the classroom as they may be viewed as being individualistic and egoistic (*wagamama* in Japanese). Or a company employee who is ambitious and seeks to move up the corporate ladder might be considered egoistic and childish. This is because the person disregards the group or *uchi* for the sake of personal interest.

In relation to Christianity, *uchi/soto* may be considered to be both beneficial and detrimental to the advance of the gospel. *Uchi/soto* may be beneficial if it promotes unity in the Church despite the different styles and denominational practices that exist within Christianity. The *uchi/soto* system could then be applied to create a strong sense of unity that emphasizes the group and the social activities of this group. However, *uchi/soto* could cause problems if the strong sense of belonging to a group hinders members of churches and ministries from reaching out to outsiders (in this case, outsiders are non-believing Japanese people and not just immigrants). The church has to realize that her doors should be open to outsiders who are willing to try Christianity.

Uchi/soto also hinders non-Christian Japanese people from accepting Christianity since it has always been considered a *soto* faith, a Western religion for foreigners (*gaijin*). As mentioned previously, Japanese people have a strong sense of duty to their group. Therefore, Christianity could pose a threat to these existing *uchi* groups. In Japan, it is vital in social interaction to use suitable etiquette and to behave appropriately. To do this, it is essential to assess the situation correctly, particularly the status of the other party (Lebra, 1976). It is especially crucial to correctly determine whether the other party is *uchi* or *soto*. According to Nakane Chie, once a person belongs to group, it is important that they do not change it too often or else their loyalty will be questioned (Nakane, 1973).

In his book, *The Day the Lord Arose*, Takimoto Jun, a Japanese pastor and author, writes concerning evangelism and new converts in his town Shinshiro:

There is a large fight involved when a citizen believes in the Lord Jesus Christ and confesses faith with Him. If somebody in a family becomes a Christian, he or she almost always meets up with the criticism of the entire family. When you try to stand as a Christian the harsh reality that waits for you is that you will have to overcome persecution. If a son or daughter becomes a Christian, sometimes the parents come to the church, crying to complain, begging, 'If my daughter becomes a Christian, we won't be able to survive in our village anymore. Please, have the pastor tell her to quit Christianity.' We are in a very difficult position at times like this. There are also frequently times when the entire family will come running into the church screaming. When believing the Lord in the midst of all of this, you have to be ready sometimes for geographic isolation, or even for being ostracized from your village ("village" refers to the neighborhood groupings that dot the city of Shinshiro—each has its own shrine, its own festival, and its own color). The custom of 'neighborhood group meetings' is deeply rooted in Shinshiro. Together with administrative business, there are many religious events, including weddings and funerals that are also conducted as part of this group. In addition, contributions for the neighborhood shrines are also gathered through this administrative system (Takimoto, 2005).

Once again, we see that due to the formation of groups (in this case the neighborhood is *uchi*) and the expected obligations of these groups, it is hard for people to choose a new lifestyle, especially a devoted Christian life. This may even be the case for most companies. As mentioned earlier, companies hesitate to employ people who are active members of a religious group. This is because it is thought that since they are already a committed member of a religious group they will not be completely devoted to the company.

Giri

Giri describes Japanese social and ethical obligations. Davies and Ikeno (2002) state that *giri* is "a key concept in understanding Japanese culture and certain characteristic patterns of behavior among the Japanese arising from traditional attitudes toward moral duty and social obligation."

Giri refers to the obligation a person has toward another person in the community. Everybody in Japanese society has some form of *giri*. *Giri* depends on two important factors: the person and their function or position and the situation in which the person is involved at a certain time and place. *Giri* is an onerous requirement on people. According to Benedict, *giri* involves various obligations. There is no equivalent concept in English. Of all the strange categories of moral obligation that anthropologists have found in the cultures of the world, *giri* is one of the most curious. It is unique to Japan.

"To an occidental," Benedict writes, "*giri* includes a most heterogeneous list of obligations ranging from gratitude for an old kindness to duty of revenge" (ibid). Benedict suggests that even Japanese dictionaries struggle to define it; one dictionary defines it as a "righteous way; the road human beings should follow; something one does unwillingly to forestall apology to the world" (ibid). The word 'unwillingly' is critical here: a Japanese person may perform a favor unwillingly, out of a sense of duty since they are expected to perform *giri*. This can be very confusing for foreigners who visit Japan. *Giri* is entailed in various relationships including student/master and employee/employer relationships. *Giri* operates both vertically and horizontally in a hierarchy.

Giri requires a person to fulfill various expectations and duties. Not performing these duties will cause the person to lose face and bring shame. However, if someone fails to perform the duty expected of them, others should continue to perform their duty or *giri* toward that person.

Since a *giri* relationship involves the continual creation of new duties and expectations, it can be prolonged indefinitely. *Giri* is not a special form of material considerations, rather it is more an affective oriented duty. Social interactions in all cultures generally tend to be egocentric; however, people in Japan are expected to express some affection toward others even if it does not come from the heart and is not genuine. *Giri* is strongly influenced by the hierarchical consciousness of the participants. This definitely has its origins in the strict social classification imposed on Japanese people during the 250 years of the Tokugawa regime.

Finally, a person with *giri* is not constrained by any behavioral ethics or codes. Therefore, if someone does not perform their duty, they violate their own sense of *giri* and will feel ashamed. Thus, there is no need to impose sanctions on them. *Giri* is rooted in Confucian ethics and social and behavioral conventions. Confucianism deals with human interrelations and interactions; it does not involve supernatural beings in any way. Human beings are obligated to each other and not to any god.

Giri could be manifested in various ways in Christian organizations and churches. *Giri* could be used to instill a sense of obligation in Christians toward non-Christians in Japan. Japanese should be trained and taught that it is their duty to evangelize their fellow Japanese by, for example, through providing social services and support such as helping the elderly or educational programs for the youth. On an individual level, *giri* toward non-Christian people should be motivated by affection and love. From the other perspective, it is very difficult for non-Christians to relinquish existing *giri* relationships and form Christ-based *giri*-oriented social relations and interactions. In this case, *giri* could be viewed as a stronghold and barrier to Christianity.

Amae

Amae, which can be roughly translated as dependence on the benevolence of others, is a key concept for understanding the Japanese personality. *Amae* is vital for getting along with others in Japan and is the basis for maintaining harmonious relationships in which children depend on their parents, younger people rely on their elders, grandparents depend on their adult children, and so on (Davies and Ikeno, 2002).

The concept of *amae* greatly affects all aspects of Japanese life because it is strongly connected with concepts such as *giri*. Due to *amae*, Japanese find it difficult to say "No" or to directly reject or disagree with someone. People hesitate to refuse others for fear of breaking the relationship, offending the person, or hurting their feelings. This may disturb the group *wa*, which can be described as unity and harmony—the desire to be one with those of your group. *Wa* is a concept that, while recognizing that people are not one, expresses the desire to be one. In other words, although people are different individuals, in Japanese culture, it is generally best when they want the same thing. This deep level of sharing underpins the desire for harmony in interpersonal relations and the consideration of others in the group. *Amae* is thus strongly related to *wa*. *Amae* is meant to create a deep emotional bonds with others in the group, but it also creates distance from others outside the group. Therefore, Japanese generally do not welcome outsiders and may even be cold toward them.

Below is an example of how *amae* works. It is taken from a book written in Dutch, whose English title is *Women Breaks Loose: The Many Faces of Japan*, by Kjeld Duits, a Dutch journalist who has lived in Japan for many years:

> *"18 year old Naomi K. describes her relationship with her boyfriend, "Whenever we walk down the street together, I want him to hold my hand." However, her sense of amae makes it difficult for her to take the first step and hold his hand. She wants to be one with him, but he has to read her feelings and hold her hand. "I would not take the initiative and hold his hand. I want him to do so. I cannot ask him directly to hold my hand, but I give him discrete signs to encourage him to take the first step. I tug his jacket a bit or give him a soft nudge." Naomi also wants him to phone her. She waits and waits. "If he does not*

give me a call, then I'll be forced to call him," she explains. "But I want him to call me and ask me out to go shopping. So, I will not call him and will not ask him to go out. I will wait. I want him to read between the lines what I want and desire" (Duits, 2002).

Another example is the indirect and understated negotiation style of the Japanese business person, which is still quite typical and well known. The Japanese are unwilling to say "No." In particular, often when they say "Yes," they actually mean "No." Lewis gives the example that if you say to a Japanese, "I want you to lend me a hundred dollars," they will mostly likely say "Yes," without actually offering the money. What they mean is, "Yes, you want me to lend you a hundred dollars." When they do not wish to make a deal with a foreign partner, they will generally not give a negative response. However, you will not be able to get in touch with your contact in that company thereafter. He or she will always be ill, on holiday, or attending a funeral (Lewis, 1996). Japanese like doing business in a harmonious environment. They do not like to offend their business partner by directly disagreeing or refusing. Japanese seldom criticize each other or even third parties and they never say "No" directly. Excessive frankness is thus usually out of place when negotiating with Japanese business persons (ibid).

Amae can be frustrating for the recipient of *amae* with all its vague and confusing signs. A 65 year old office manager explains how he and his colleagues would rack their brains to find out what their boss wanted them to do:

On a hot summer day, if the boss says, 'It's hot today', we begin to ask ourselves, 'What we should do?' If someone is courageous enough, he may turn the air conditioning on. If the boss does not show any reaction or makes comments expressing his irritation, then we know he was not implying that we should turn the air conditioning on. In that case, someone will open the window, and if that does not work then someone will give him an iced tea (Duits, 2002).

This process would continue indefinitely until they discover what their boss really wanted. In some cases, *amae* goes against some

Christian values. For instance, Jesus said in the Bible, "Simply let your 'Yes' be 'Yes,' and your 'No,' 'No'; anything beyond this comes from the evil one" (Matthew 5:37) (here, Christianity does not refer to Western culture, but to pure Christian doctrine based on what the Bible teaches). Directness and clarity are values of the Christian faith. This is the opposite of *amae*. Imagine evangelizing someone who says "Yes", but means "No." I consider *amae* to be a stronghold since it makes people captive to the group and unable to express their true convictions. It can even be a stronghold within the church. If *amae* is consciously or unconsciously used in churches and Christian fellowships in Japan, it will be hard to reach unbelievers. Could this be one reason why the church in Japan is not growing?

Aimai

Aimai means 'ambiguity;' this occurs when there is more than one possible meaning and results in obscurity, indistinctness, and uncertainty. To be ambiguous is generally translated as *aimai* in Japanese, but the term has a wide range of meanings including 'vague, obscure, equivocal, dubious, doubtful, questionable, shady, noncommittal, indefinite, hazy, double, two-edged,' and so on (Davies and Ikeno, 2002). *Aimai* is an ancient communication strategy for Japanese people that has its roots in the need for harmony. As mentioned earlier, Japan was cut off from the outside world during the Tokugawa period. Consequently, communities depended on each other to produce food. Collectively, they had to work and cooperate in harmony in order to produce more. To achieve this they practiced *aimai*. Natural communication often occurred without spoken words, and people followed their elders because they had more experience, wisdom, and power. In order to live without creating any serious problems for the group's harmony, people avoided expressing their ideas clearly, even to the point of avoiding giving a simple yes or no answer. If a person really wanted to say "No", he or she said nothing at first and then used vague expressions that conveyed the nuance of disagreement (Davies and Ikeno, 2002).

Another reason for ambiguity is the feeling that to speak directly is to assume superiority over the person you are conversing with. The Japanese think it is impolite to speak openly since it implies that their partner is ignorant. The Japanese value *aimai* because they think that it is unnecessary to speak clearly if their partner is knowledgeable. Silence can also be considered a form of ambiguity. For the Japanese, silence indicates deep thinking or consideration, whereas long periods of silence often make non-Japanese uncomfortable.

Once again, we see that being indirect and not sharing your true feelings but following the interests of the group is very important. In the case of *aimai*, the speaker assumes that the listener already knows what they want to say even if the listener does not fully understand what is said. This makes the listener coequal with the speaker; if someone explains everything in detail they may come across as being arrogant and proud. This makes evangelism very challenging as it means assuming that the listeners already know Christ and the good news of the gospel. Some evangelists, especially from North America or Europe, go to Japan with the attitude that they are coming to teach, that they know better, that they have it all, and that their own style of worship and ministry is the best one. This attitude makes evangelists and missionaries appear *wagamama*—childish and selfish.

However, I still consider *aimai* as a stronghold because the Christian message is a direct message and cultural values such as hinder the clear proclamation of the gospel of Christ. For this reason, outsiders going to Japan for the purpose of evangelism (and even Japanese Christians) should aim to be direct in their message and lifestyle. Christian leaders and pastors and those in authority need to teach Japanese Christians the basic principles of why it is important to be direct and how directness can help when witnessing to an unbeliever.

Sempai / Kohai

Sempai/kohai basically refers to rules and regulations based on seniority. In Japan, vertical relationships are more important than horizontal relationships. Seniors are called sempai and they address their juniors as *kohai*.

Vertical hierarchies have existed since the beginning of Japanese history and they are still prevalent in daily life, especially in schools that emphasize rules based on seniority. For example, third-year students have great power in junior high and senior high schools, especially in extracurricular clubs. It is common in sports clubs for *kohai* to clean the rooms, collect balls, and manage the equipment for *sempai*. They must also give a small bow or say hello respectfully to their *sempai* when greeting them. Japanese students generally place much more importance on age than ability. Seniority rules also influence relationships between teachers and students (Davies and Ikeno, 2002).

Rules based on seniority are also important in companies or institutions. The seniority system and the lifetime employment system are the foundations of life in Japanese companies, although it remains to be seen whether these frameworks will survive. Status, position, and salary depend largely on seniority, and older employees are generally in higher positions and are paid more than their younger subordinates (ibid). However, as discussed above, the lifetime employment system is slowly disappearing and it is unclear whether the seniority culture will survive in another form; only time will tell.

The *sempai/kohai* system has advantages when it is practiced properly. However, it is sometimes abused, occasionally in the most extreme and inhumane ways. This abuse is particularly prevalent at schools and gives rise to bullying in which seniors abuse the juniors. Kjeld Duits gives a very horrible description of one such case of abuse:

Ichiro's dream came true when he was accepted at a prestigious high school in West Japan. Ichiro's ambition was to become a professional athlete in kendo, a Japanese martial art involving sword fighting. The school that he attended has a good reputation for this sport. However, the dreams of this young man turned into a terrible nightmare from which it was very hard for him to escape. After a month of attending that school, his mother began to notice blue marks and bruises on his knees and back. She commented on them, but her son did not reply or he would say that he had fallen during practice.

A month later, Ichiro returned home from a sports competition perplexed and shocked by what he had seen in the changing room of the sports center. Three of the juniors in the team of five live in the same dormitory as the seniors. He explained how the seniors sexually and brutally harassed these three boys. [Duits described the details, which I do not find appropriate to describe in this book.]

Ichiro told one of the boys that he should speak to his parents, but the boy strongly refused because of what might happen to him. Within a few months, the juniors on the team began to speak about ending their misery by committing suicide. When the story reached some of the parents, the parents went to the school and protested. One of the mothers begged and pleaded with the coach and yet it did not help at all. Instead, the coach laughed at her and ironically said, "The times have so changed that even parents are coming to tell me these things." Then he addressed all the parents and said. "If I stop this bullying, your kids will never win any competition." The parents begged for two hours and yet the coach did not show any sympathy and even ridiculed the parents (Duits, 2002).

Most of such incidents take place in high schools. No wonder some kids become *hikikomori*, isolating themselves for years. This incident reveals how *sempai/kohai* can have a negative effect.

Wa

According to Harold Perkin, "*Wa* does not seek to embody itself in individual rights or concrete rational law. From the individual's point of view it is an emotional attachment to the group—the family, community, working team, firm, nation—and an expectation that effort, cooperation, and loyalty will be rewarded by the group's permanent concern for one's welfare" (Perkin, 1996). In other words, although people are distinct individuals, in Japanese culture, it is generally best if they want the same thing. This deep level of sharing underpins the desire for harmony in interpersonal relations and the consideration of other member of the group. According to Joy Hendry, *wa* is sometimes used to stand for Japan or Japaneseness (Hendry, 2004). In this context of *wa*, most Japanese might feel that if they become a Christian they will relinquish some of their Japaneseness and abandon the group *wa*. Christians can be perceived as being antisocial and selfish because they disrupt the harmony of the family unit by refusing to observe many traditional Shinto and Buddhist rituals, especially those involving praying to spirits and reverencing the dead (ibid).

The root of corporatism is found in the concept of *wa* or harmony. Japanese social life is based on corporatism driven by *wa*. Japanese culture and social life are both centered on this concept of harmony with others, both the living and deceased; harmony with gods as well as with nature is central here. Generally, the Japanese do not distinguish between the human and the divine or between the living and the dead. As Anthony Failow wrote in the Washington Post:

> *In Japan, wa surrounds you. You can feel it in the priciest sushi bars and lowliest noodle parlors. Call it the particular Japanese way of looking at the world: of harmony, of collectiveness with do-not-rock-the- boat spirit. In the mythology of the 'Star wars movies, the wa is like the Force. To mess with the wa is a cardinal sin.*[1]

The concept of *wa* was adapted in Japan's first constitution called *Prince Shotoku's Seventeen Article Constitution* or *Jushichijo Kenpo* and promulgated by Prince Shotoku in 604.[2]   In Japan, group harmony

---

1 - Japanese Society: Wa, Confucianism, Homogeneity, Conformity, Individualism and Hierarchies," last modified March 2012, http://factsanddetails.com/japan. php?itemid=642&catid=18.

2 - The first article was as follows: Harmony should be valued and quarrels should be avoided. Everyone has his biases, and few men are far-sighted. Therefore some disobey their lords and fathers and keep up feuds with their neighbors. But when the superiors are in harmony with each other and the inferiors are friendly, then affairs are discussed quietly and the right view of matters prevails. http://www.sarudama.com/japanese _history/jushichijokenpo.shtml

means that a person knows his/her place in the social hierarchy and behaves accordingly. It also means that one has to keep silent even if one is unhappy or upset about something, just for the sake of not disturbing the harmony or *wa*. *Wa* tends to take precedence over individual autonomy, and self-reliance is recognized as a virtue only insofar as it aids in the creation of social harmony (Dale, 1996). Mullins writes:

> *In the Japanese context, Christianity and many new religions encourage individuals to consider alternative interpretations of reality, lifestyles, and spiritual disciplines. As a result, these new traditions can cause conflict and division in many situations and be disruptive of the wa, or harmony, of traditional Japanese society (Mullins, 1998).*

During his presentation at the 2010 Tokyo Global Mission Consultation, Minoru Okuyama, the director of the Missionary Training Center in Japan, stated that the Japanese are afraid of disturbing the human relationships within their families or neighborhoods by becoming Christian. Okuyama emphasized that one of the most important things in Japan is *wa*— those who disturb it are regarded as bad, irrespective of whether they are right or wrong (VU, 2010). Therefore, it is quite hard for a Japanese to decide to become a Christian, for his/her choice means disturbing that harmony (Davies & Ikeno, 2002). Disturbing the group by being too individualistic or out of step with others is considered selfish.

Finally

There are many other important elements in Japanese culture. I chose only a few of them to describe here. I hope these examples illustrate how important it is to understand Japanese culture before trying to evangelize Japanese. The next chapter deals with some important spiritual customs in Japan such as festivals and the beliefs related to these festivals.

Chapter Thirteen

Spiritual Culture in Japan

Every culture has its own spiritual beliefs and ways of thinking along with important days and traditions. This chapter describes such beliefs in Japan and important cultural and spiritual festivals.

Matsuri : Important Traditional Festivals

The word *matsuri* means 'festival.' Various festivals are celebrated in Japan. Some are nationwide while others are local. *Matsuri* comes from the word *matsu*, which means to welcome the invisible to the visible world. *Matsuri* have two aspects—contact with invisible spirits and contact with living people. Below, I explain some important *matsuri* or festivals in Japanese culture.

Obon Festival

This festival is celebrated according to the lunar calendar. *Obon*, the festival of souls, is held in mid-July or mid-August depending on the area. It is believed that each year on *Obon* day, ancestors' spirits return to this world to visit their relatives. Lanterns are traditionally hung in front of houses to guide the ancestors' spirits. People visit the graves of their relatives and offer food at house altars or in temples. Special dances are performed on this day. Streets are decorated with lanterns and at the end of *Obon* floating lanterns are placed on rivers, lakes, and the sea to guide the spirits back to their world. The customs followed vary significantly from region to region.

Setsubun

Setsubun is held on February 3 or 4. Each year on this day people open the doors of their homes and drive demons and bad luck out of their homes by throwing roasted soybeans in their homes and shouting, *"Fuku wa uchi, oni wa soto,"* which means, "In with good luck! Out with demons!"

It originally started as an imperial event on New Year's Eve with the purpose of getting rid of demons and welcoming in the new year. It was later combined with the indigenous custom of throwing soybeans at the time of planting rice seedlings and it has thus evolved into its present form (Katayama, 2004).

Hina matsuri

Hina matsuri is a girls' or doll festival. This festival is celebrated on March 3 when the birth of girls is celebrated and wishes are expressed for their future happiness. *Hina matsuri* is the day on which *hina ningyo,* sets of dolls dressed in ancient costumes, are displayed together with peach blossoms as decorations. The dolls represent the members of the imperial court of ten centuries ago. At the top of the display, two dolls represent the Emperor and the Empress. Some of these dolls cost thousands of dollars. A sweet drink made from rice called *shirozake* is offered. Japanese people believe that the dolls have souls. Most Japanese people will never place a doll in a bedroom since the doll could perform strange things during the night (Duits, 2002).

Some dolls used in *Hina matsuri* are passed from generation to generation and some are a few hundred years old, making them extremely valuable. The girls of the family inherit them. Many such dolls were destroyed during World War II, particularly in Hiroshima. Consequently, the doll industry boomed after the war and some doll makers made a lot of money.

The Japanese people value dolls so much that they either give them to someone or pass them on to the next generation; they never throw a doll away. The dolls are kept in a special place in temples. Some are placed in small wooden boats and are released on to the ocean because they are thought to take away bad luck, illness, uncleanness, and negativity. Other dolls are burned in temples in a ceremony that is similar to a cremation ceremony (ibid). Thus, dolls provide emotional healing for the Japanese and they resemble little saviors since they take away guilt, negativity, and bad luck. This is what the Japanese believe!

Most families take their beautiful collection of dolls out of the closet around mid-February and put them away again as soon as *Hinamatsuri* is over. This is because of an old superstition that families that are slow in putting back the dolls back have trouble marrying off their daughters. Girls are cherished during *Hina matsuri* and they receive attention from their parents and family who pray for their wellbeing.

Tango no Sekku

Tango no Sekku is an event rooted in ancient times, which is celebrated on Children's Day (May 5). People express the hope that each boy in the family will grow up strong and healthy by flying carp-shaped streamers outside their homes and displaying a warrior doll. This custom was developed by the warrior class during the feudal period and it was also observed by civilians of the time in a different way. Women are considered superior to men on that day. For example, women may take a bath before men and men prepare meals for women (Katayama, 2004). This is very ironic in view of the changes that are occurring in modern Japanese society and how women are viewed in Japan.

Some Modern Day Events

With the introduction of Western culture to Japan after World War II, some Western cultural events such as Christmas and Valentine's Day have become very important in Japan. Christmas was initially introduced to Japan with the arrival of the first Europeans in the 16th century. But only in recent decades has it enjoyed wide popularity in Japan. This is despite the fact that Christians make up only about 2% of the population. While Christmas is not a national holiday in Japan, more and more people decorate their homes, give presents to friends, and celebrate the event with a special meal. In a survey conducted by

'Japan-guide.com', 54% of young Japanese people said that Christmas means something special to them. Women and teenagers show particular interest in Christmas. However, the greatest enthusiasm for Christmas comes from retail stores and shopping malls where Christmas trees, Santa Clauses, and seasonal decorations are displayed several weeks prior to Christmas. Some public places also feature seasonal illuminations. The traditional Christmas food in Japan is the Christmas cake, which is usually made of sponge cake, strawberries, and whipped cream. As many as 73% of Japanese celebrate Christmas with a cake.[1]

Valentine's Day is also celebrated in Japan. Women buy chocolates for the one they love or like, but they are also expected to buy *giri choco* (literally, obligation chocolate) for their male colleagues. Also, fathers and husbands receive chocolates from girls or women. One month later on March 14, men are expected to do the same thing for women. This day is called White Day. Men buy white chocolates for women and some women also receive white underwear! Men give chocolates only to those women from whom they received something on Valentine's Day a month earlier.

Fortune Telling in Japan

Japan is a fortune-telling nation. The fortune-telling business is growing rapidly and various new forms of fortune-telling are now being invented. Fortune tellers can be seen in the streets and near subway stations. More and more people consult fortune tellers for various reasons: some seek guidance about business decisions, some want to find the right partner, and some want guidance in their careers. People in Japan are searching for answers, especially during this time when the nation is undergoing gradual but radical social-economic and cultural changes. Uncertainty about the future is one reason for the booming fortune-telling business. I have also discovered that people avoid going to professional psychiatrists because they are

1 - www.japan-guide.com

afraid of losing face among their relatives and friends. Instead, they consult fortune tellers and they may even base their lives on what fortune tellers tell them.

Finally

The Japanese festivals of inviting invisible spirits to bless their daughters and sons do not appear to be very effective since many children are bullied at schools and between 500,000 and 1,000,000 young people are isolated as *hikikomori*. The next chapter deals with various socio-cultural problems. These problems are culturally and socially related to each other and they cause Japanese society to become less healthy. Japanese people appear to be searching for something new—for answers. I hope the church and Christianity will provide these answers. May the church provide biblical and ethical solutions for the searching Japanese men and women.

Analysis & Strategies

Summary

Japan is a fascinating nation. It is a society full of mystery and surprises, at least for people who view this nation from a distance (particularly Westerners).

Part 1 described some important aspects of Japan, beginning with its formation and theories concerning its origin. It gave an overview of general Japanese history and also the history of Christianity in this nation from early times through to the present. The commonly accepted origin of the Japanese people, namely the Jomon people, was explained. In addition, the mythological view of the origin of Japan was discussed since it plays an important role in Japanese culture and society. I did not reject the theory of Japan being one of the lost tribes of Israel or a mixture of Asian and Jewish or Middle Eastern cultures. The resemblance between some Japanese festivals and Jewish customs was discussed. The historical overview focused on two main periods: the Tokugawa period (1603–1868) and the Meiji period (1868–1912). During the Tokugawa period, Japan was isolated from the outside world. Besides the Dutch, Japan did not cooperate with any other nation. In addition, society was stratified into classes. The national religion was Buddhism in conjunction with a strong emphasis on Confucian ethics. Christianity was regarded as a major threat during this period and it was systematically eliminated. Christians were persecuted and publicly killed. Some Christians managed to maintain their faith secretly for a couple of centuries until they were discovered in the Meiji period.

Part 2 focused on modern Japanese society. It described important elements of Japanese society such as the role of the individual, family, work, gender stratification, and minorities. It also discussed social issues that threaten the structure of society such as the low birth rate and the fatherless society.

Parts 3 & 4 described Japanese views on religion in general as well as the history of Christianity in Japan. Part 5 described Japanese culture and some basic cultural concepts such as *honne/tatemae, uchi/soto, giri, amae, aimai,* and *wa,* which all have significant implications for Christianity. The effect of these factors on the Christian faith and how they make it difficult for Christianity to spread in Japan were considered. Also, some socio-cultural problems such as sexual immorality, social protest, suicide, and homelessness in Japan were briefly discussed.

Analysis

Japan is a superpower on the edge of moral and social decay. It is a nation searching for answers and it lacks a moral compass. How can Christians influence this society and what are suitable strategies for reintroducing Christianity to Japan?

I personally believe that Christianity has not been introduced properly to Japan. Christianity should be reintroduced in Japan and Christian scholars and ministers should prayerfully find new strategies for giving Christianity another image. Before discussing some potential strategies for evangelizing Japan, we first examine some crucial factors that have prevented Christianity from spreading in Japan. These factors can be categorized into three major factors: historical factors, socio-cultural factors, and church factors.

Historical Factors

Christianity has been considered a Western religion, which was from the very beginning connected to the colonialism and imperialism of the 1500s. Christianity posed a political threat to Japan. It was considered the religion of an enemy that desired to infiltrate Japan. After modernization and the introduction of freedom of religion during the Meiji period, some Christians made the crucial mistake of entering Japan with a Western mindset. They attempted to impose

Western culture on the Japanese. This hindered the growth of Christianity in Japan. After the US defeated Japan in World War II by employing the atomic bomb, the Allied forces forced the emperor to acknowledge that he was not a god; this caused some Japanese people to dislike Christianity, viewing it as the religion of the Americans who had shamefully defeated them.

Cultural Factors

Cultural factors are very crucial. The following are some cultural factors that have hindered the growth of Christianity in Japan. First, Shinto, the native Japanese religion, is polytheistic. The Japanese concept of gods differs completely from the God of the Christian faith. In Japan, gods are considered as being neither good nor bad. Furthermore, the gods or *kami* are not personal; they do not relate to people. Keep them satisfied and content and they will not harm you or bring calamities. The opposite is true in Christianity. God is the supreme creator, kind compassionate, all knowing, and loving. He does not require religious rituals to keep Him happy. He is a God who is full of grace.

Another cultural factor is the concept of sin and the fallenness of humanity. In Japanese culture, man is good by nature. However, worldly attachments are bad and they make a person corrupt. This can be fought by controlling and minimizing the selfish desires that may lead to childishness (*wagamama*). Also, the word Japanese for "sin" is the same word used for "crime" so that only criminals, thieves, and killers are sinners; the average Japanese person does not consider themselves a sinner. In other words, the concept of sin and fallen man is completely different to the biblical doctrine. When an evangelist tells a Japanese person that they are a sinner, they do not understand because they do not consider themselves criminals.

The Japanese are shame-oriented rather than sin-oriented people. In Bible, man is created in the image of God, but since the fall of man all people are evil by nature. Sin is considered to be disobeying the Lord's commands and rejecting God's Son as Lord and Savior.

This brings us to a third cultural factor that prevents the spread of the gospel: forgiveness. Since there is no proper concept of sin, it is difficult to understand God's forgiveness in the Christian faith. In Japanese culture, if a wrong has been committed, there must be some way to make it good. If there is no way to make restitution, then the offender and their family will endure endless shame and guilt. n Christianity, however, there is no other way to compensate and make good with God. The only one way is through accepting Christ as Lord. He alone can take away our guilt and shame through His grace and mercy.

A fourth reason is that the Japanese are group-oriented people. They think in terms of *uchi/soto* and they have to do all they can for the interests of their group rather than for their own interests. They do to avoid losing face with the group, which brings dire consequences. For example, the local neighborhood is considered to be an *uchi* group. Every neighborhood group organizes activities that include religious activities and rituals. Therefore, if someone starts attending church they may be considered a threat to the neighborhood. This will bring shame on their family. This will become more intense if a person decides to be baptized. Since Japan is a ceremony-oriented nation, baptism can be considered a betrayal of the national culture of Japan. Consequently, some parents do all they can to stop their newly converted children from being baptized.

The fifth cultural reason is that the Japanese consider Christians to be childish because Christians claim there is only one way to God— Jesus Christ. The Japanese considers this arrogant.

Finally, Japanese society is a work-oriented society to the extent that work is often considered to be more important than the family. As mentioned earlier, I consider Japan to be a company-worshiping nation. Therefore, church and church activities may reduce a person's loyalty to their work or company. Since people think that going to church on Sundays makes a person a Christian, they are reluctant to even consider becoming a Christian because they are afraid to lose their only free day. Attending church would be an obligation or *giri*. Many other factors could be discussed, but I consider the above reasons to be sufficient for the present purposes.

Church Factors

By church factors, I mean that there are certain responsibilities the Church has to change society. The Church should represent itself better to the rapidly transforming global society, including Japan. I believe that there should be a distinction between the Church and Western culture. The Church has failed to represent itself as a 'culture–free' faith and as an independent faith. Missionaries and Christians from other countries did not fully investigate the nation and the culture to build a bridge of trust and understanding. I have interviewed believers in Japan and other Asian nations. They consider the Western style of Christianity to be very aggressive and dominant. They claim that Westerners come with the attitude, "We know better than you and we have come to teach you, the Japanese Christians, something." This goes totally against the culture in which timidity, silence, calmness, and humbleness are considered important virtues.

Another factor is that the church should relate more to society and address current issues in society. The church has to offer solutions to various questions and concerns. The church forms a group and lives a group life on its own. However, the church should come out of group life and begin to connect with other people.

Finally, Christian leadership has not kept up with the latest developments in technology, art, and science. This makes the church appear old fashioned and boring to the average Japanese person. The church should be closer to the people and society.

Strategies and Suggestions

Japan is changing. The family, youth, the elderly, the educational system, labor management, and the economy are changing drastically and there are major crises in some areas. This book has mentioned some of these crises.

Families are becoming increasingly fatherless. Mothers and children have to find their own way to survive in a merciless and rapidly changing society. Most churches are old fashioned and are not keeping up with the rapid developments in technology. Pastors are aging: their average age is 60. Many think that most churches will close in 20 years. However, I also mentioned that the Pentecostal and charismatic forms of Christianity are growing faster. There are not many of these churches but they can grow and think up new strategies for reaching Japan with the gospel of Jesus Christ. Below, I share my suggested strategies for the Church in Japan.

Total Transformation of the Christian Message

Japanese culture is a very complicated set of dualistic contradictions. Japanese people often say "Yes" when they actually mean "No." They have to suppress their inner feelings in order to maintain harmony in the family or group by being politically correct. Unfortunately, many Christians in Japan have grown up with this way of thinking and society pressures them to act this way. Japanese Christians are often made to feel that faith and belief are personal issues and that it is childish or impolite to express your views to someone else.

Cultural elements, such as *honne/tatemae, amae, and aimai,* remain strongholds. Modern Christianity should address these cultural issues and teach Christians to openly express their ideas and feelings publicly, which goes against mainstream culture. This means that evangelistic efforts should not be limited by the culture but should change the culture to express the Christian message. By doing this, Christians have to find ways to bring the gospel to the hearts of every Japanese. For instance, the Internet has allowed suffering woman to bypass the existing neighborhood culture of control by creating online forums that allow them to openly share their experiences without loosing face in the neighborhood or in the family. Such women often use pseudonyms and are very open about their inner feelings, which they find difficult to share in normal environments. I have heard that many women have been helped through such forums, groups, and discussion sites. Sending text messages on mobile phones is very effective because many Japanese can express their feelings better through texting by mobile phone than by face-to-face interactions.

Can we Christians use such methods to reach the Japanese with the gospel of Jesus Christ?

On the other hand, I believe we need to redefine our understanding of Christianity and the church as an organization. I believe that the church as an established organization with buildings, elders, deacons, and religious structures will not be able to reach the Japanese people. Operation World 2010 states that, "the impact of the Japanese Church is inadequate. The Church must turn from its insular, bunker mentality to engage with society. The government is not adequately solving the social ills confronting Japan; the transforming power of Christ, as expressed through a revived church, is an answer not being adequately offered. There is, however, a new emphasis on evangelism in many churches and a willingness to try new paradigms of ministry" (Mandryk, 2010).

Further, there should be an alternative for new Japanese converts to live out their faith without being expelled from their neighborhood communities or families. Will it be possible that postmodern Japanese society will embrace Christianity in a different form, a new way in which technology, social care, and community play an increasingly important role? Will it be possible to create a community of Japanese Christians who do not have to attend church every Sunday and yet are active Christians in the marketplace and society? These are the questions that only time will answer. Christianity has a lot to offer during this time when so many Japanese lack direction.

Lastly, new ways of doing church need to be realized. Operation World suggests that nonessential forms of the church must be modified to look less like the introduced Western culture of years past and more like 21st century Japan. House churches may be a good alternative for those who are uncomfortable with being a part of a traditional church (Mandryk, 2010). In addition, I hope that the Japanese will revive the Non-Church Movement in a form that is more suitable for contemporary Japanese society. I personally believe that reviving the Non-Church Movement and reintroducing Japan's native theologians from the past by modifying their ideas to the current situation in Japan will be very effective for reaching the Japanese people with the gospel.

Reaching the Youth

Another strategy for the church is to reach the youth. How can the church reach the youth effectively when the average age of leaders in Japan is 60? Young people are suffering from problems such as suicide, *hikikomori*, anger against the establishment, bullying, incest, harsh educational system, other people's expectations, and prostitution.

According to Operation World 2010, young people between 18 and 23 are the most open to the gospel. 85% of Japanese teenagers wonder why they exist, while 11% wish they had never been born (Mandryk, 2010). Thus, young people urgently need help. Most churches do not offer deep and effective outreach to these youth. I suggest that churches should seek digital means for reaching the youth. Strong Internet services are needed to reach the Japanese youth. Websites, forums, and chatting services should create a friendly atmosphere and provide assistance.

Another crisis that the youth face is that of finding a proper spouse. Japanese youth are finding it difficult to find partners. I believe the Church can play a crucial role by providing Christian *miai* or Christian matchmaking agencies.

Reaching Minorities

As mentioned before, minorities such as *burakumin* and groups experience strong discrimination. These minorities are Japanese and yet they are not considered Japanese. I believe the Church should find proper strategies for reaching these minorities. When I was conducting my research and was talking informally with some Japanese Christians, I discovered that these prejudices exist even within the Christian church. Even Christians do not like to interact with people such as *burakumin*. Even Christian parents do not like their children to marry Christians with a *burakumin* or Ainu background. Christians in Japan should offer welcoming arms to these minorities.

There are also non-Japanese minorities such as the Koreans. The church is very strong in the Korean community in Japan. Koreans have bigger churches than the average Japanese church. Therefore, supporting the Korean church in Japan and Korean missionaries in Japan would be very effective since the negative image of Koreans in Japan is beginning to change. More and more Japanese women are marring Korean men. The church can use this opportunity to expose Japanese women to the gospel of Jesus Christ. Other minorities such as Filipinos are also very active in Japan, establishing fellowships and Christian communities. Nowadays, international churches are increasing in Japan. These are churches with mixed nationalities such as Filipinos, Chinese, and Koreans, Japanese, and Africans. Interaction between Japanese Christians and other Christian nationalities can create an atmosphere of unity and help reach Japan with the gospel.

Women: the Secret for Revival in Japan

As stated above, women do not enjoy a high position in Japanese society. Many women in Japan are suffering; many experience loneliness, pain, and frustrations. Culturally, they are not viewed as being equal to men, even though the law says they are! Women have been exploited for sexual pleasure and have been subjected to sexual mistreatment. Consequently, the Church should change its teaching about women. It may sound strange, but more women attend church in Japan than men. However, these women are traditionally trained to remain silent and only come to church for their own personal worship. The attitude of the Church toward Japanese women should change. There is a biblical proverb, "iron sharpens iron." Christian women in Japan should be more effectively trained and released into evangelism and counseling.

Contextualize Your Approach

Japanese culture has many beautiful aspects that can be used as contexts for presenting the Gospel. A Christian friend of mine once told me that, one day, a friend of his who was a passionate Shinto believer came to him holding a copy of the Bible. He said excitedly to my friend, "I read the Torah. I was very surprised to learn about the religious ceremonies of ancient Israel. They show similarities with Shinto ceremonies. The feasts, the structure of the tabernacle, the temple, the Ark of the Covenant, the value of cleanliness, the impurity of the dead: all of those are similar to Shinto elements!" My friend then said to him, "Yes, that is what I have also noticed. If you have discovered it, why don't you believe in God, of whom the Bible teaches?" This was the start of many interesting conversations between the two friends. I personally believe that, for example, Shinto and even Buddhism present contextual grounds that can be used as starting points for contextualization. Thankfully, there are ministers today who use the tea ceremony as a means to evangelize the Japanese. From another angle, it would be great to have more churches made stylized to appeal to religious frameworks of the Japanese. I am sure that they exist at present, though more would be even better.

Another way of implementing contextualization is to study Japanese society. By identifying various societal needs and studying their causes and roots, we may develop important contextual tools for reaching out to the Japanese people. Officiating marriage ceremonies, conducting funeral services, and offering various services to the elderly may all be considered to be contextual as well. I am sure that some ministries specialize in helping people with suicidal tendencies. These are all good examples of contextualization.

Closing Remarks

We should never forget the blood of the martyrs shed on Japanese soil. We also have to remember the courage of many Christians who kept their faith secret for almost 250 years during the Tokugawa period. I also believe that the current church should do more and seek forgiveness from God and from the Japanese people for its apathy and ignorance about the problems in society. We should ask for forgiveness for not being a part of this society and not providing enough solutions and care to this desperate people. I believe that by practicing what I have discussed in this book while carefully and strategically praying for Japan, the hearts of the Japanese people will become more open and receptive to our message. This will surely lead to a revival of the Christian faith in this nation.

I simply want this book to be a Christian sociological book, which will be used as a handbook for every person and every Christian missionary, evangelist, or pastor who wants to reach this beautiful nation with the love of Christ and not with a Western religion!

You have to love Japan in order to reach Japan.

Bibliography

Ama, Toshimaro (2004) *Why Are the Japanese Non-Religious? Japanese Spirituality: Being Non-Religious in a Religious Culture*. Lanham: University Press of America.

Bales, Kevin (2007) *Ending Slavery: How We Free Today's Slaves*. Berkeley: University of Californian Press).

Benedict, Ruth (1946) *The Chrysanthemum and the Sword: Patterns of Japanese Culture*. Boston: Houghton Mifflin Company.

Best, Ernest (1966) *Christian Faith and Cultural Crisis: the Japanese case*. Leiden: Brill.

Bowring, Richard and Kornicki, Peter (1993) *The Cambridge Encyclopedia of Japan*. Cambridge: Cambridge University Press.

Buckley, Sandra (Ed.) (2002) *Encyclopedia of Contemporary Japanese Culture*. New York: Routledge.

Burgess, Adam and Horii, Mitsutoshi (2012) "Constructing Sexual Risk: 'Chikan', Collapsing Male Authority and the Emergence of Women-Only Train Carriages in Japan" in Japan, Health, Risk & Society, 14:1, 41-55, DOI: 10.1080/13698575.2011.641523.

Clement, Ernest W. (1905) *Christianity in Modern Japan*. Philadelphia: American Baptist Publication Society.

Crawcour, Sydney (1974) "The Tokugawa period and Japan's Preparation for Modern Economic Growth" in The Journal of Japanese Studies: 1(1): 113–125.

Curtin, J. Sean (2005) "Women and Japan's New Poor." Article written for www.japan-focus.org

Davies, Roger and Ikeno, Osamu (2002) *The Japanese Mind: Understanding Contemporary Japanese culture.* Boston: Tuttle Publishing.

Duits, Kjeld (2002) *Vrouw Breekt Los: De Vele Gezichten van Japan.* (Translation from Dutch: Woman Breaks Loose: Many Faces of Japan). The Hague: Uitgeverij BZZToH.

Dziesinski, Michael J. (2003) *"Hikikomori: Investigations Into the Phenomenon of Acute Social Withdrawal in Contemporary Japan"* (paper). Honolulu: University of Hawaii, Manoa.

Endo, Shusaku (1980) *Silence.* New Jersey: Taplinger Publishing Company.

Esenbel, Selçuk (2011) *Japan, Turkey and the World of Islam: The writings of Selçuk Esenbel.* Leiden: Brill NV.

Francis, Carolyn Bowen and Nakajima, John Masaaki (1991) *Christians in Japan.* New York: Friendship Press, Inc.

Furaya, Yasuo (Editor) (1997) *A history of Japanese Theology.* Grand Rapids, Michigan: William B. Eerdmans Publishing Company.

Hall, John Whitney (1991) *Japan: Prehistory to Modern Times.* Frankfurt am Main: S. Fischer Verlag.

Harrington, Ann M. (1993) *Japan's Hidden Christians.* Chicago: Loyola University Press.

Hastings, Sally A. (2007) "Gender and Sexuality in Modern Japan" in *A Companion To Japanese History,* ed. William M. Tsutsui. Oxford: Blackwell Publishing Ltd.

Hendry, Joy (2004) *Understanding Japanese Society.* London: Routledge Curzon.

Higashibaba, Ikuo (2001) *Christianity in Early Modern Japan: Kirishitans Belief and Practice.* Leiden: Brill.

Hirata, Keiko and Warschauer, Mark (2014) *Japan: The Paradox of Harmony.* London: Yale University Press.

Howes, John F. (2005) *Japan's Modern Prophet: Uchimura Kanzo 1861–1930.* Vancouver: University of British Columbia.

Imamura, Anne E. (1990) "The Japanese Family", an article written for the Asian Society's Video Letter from Japan II: a young family, pages 7–17.

Johnstone, Patrick and Mandryk Jason (2001) *Operation World: 21st Century Edition.* Carlisle, UK: Paternoster Lifestyle.

Joseph, Ken Jr. (2001) *Lost Identity.* Tokyo: The Keikyo Institute.

Kambayashi, Takehiko (2004) "Japan's Homeless Face Ageism" (article, 18 October 2004) in The Christian Science Monitor (www.scmonitor.com)

Kapner, Daniel Ari and Levine, Stephen (2000) "The Jews of Japan" in Jerusalem Letter, No. 425, 1 March 2000.

Katayama, Patricia Mari (Editor) (2004) *Talking about Japan: Q and A.* Third Edition. Tokyo: Bilingual Books.

Kingston, Jeff (2010) *Contemporary Japan: History, Politics, and Social Change Since 1980s.* West Sussex: Wiley-Blackwell.

Kubo, Arimasa (1999) *Lost Tribes-Japan: Israelites came to Japan.* Tokyo: Remnant Publishing.

Lande, Aasulv (1989) *Meiji Protestantism in History and Historiography.* Frankfurt am Main: Verlag Peter Lang GmbH.

Lebra, T. Sugiyama (1976) *Japanese Patterns of Behavior.* Honolulu: University of Hawaii Press.

Lee, Shiu Keung (1971) *The Cross and the Lotus.* Hong Kong: Christian Study Center on Chinese Religion and Culture.

Lewis, R.D. (1996) *When Culture Collide: Managing Successfully Across Cultures.* London: Nicholas Brealey.

Li, Yuk Heung (1993) *Woman's Education in Meiji Japan and Development of Christian Girls' School.* Hong Kong: University of Hong Kong.

Masako, Ishii-Kuntz (2004) "Japanese Fathers' Involvement in Childcare, A Power point Presentation". University of California, Riverside: Department of Sociology.

Mandryk, Jason (2010) *Operation World: The Definitive Prayer Guide to Every Nation*. Completely Revised -7th Edition. Colorado Springs: Biblica Publishing.

Mastumoto, David (2002) *The New Japan: Debunking Seven Cultural Stereotypes*. Yarmouth: Intercultural Press, Inc.

McDowell, Josh (1994) *Christianity: A Ready Defense*. San Bernardino: Here's Life Publishing Inc.

Meyvis, Ludo and Vande Walle, Willy (1989) *Japan: Het Onvoltooide Experiment*. Translation from Dutch: (Japan: the Unfinished Experiment). Tielt: Drukkerij- Uitgeverij Lanno.

Michelson, Carl (1960) *Japanese Contributions to Christian Theology*. Philadelphia: Westminster Press.

Moni, Monir Hossain (2004) "Christianity's Failure to Thrive in Today's Japan" (paper) Tokyo: Hitotsubashi University, Dept. of International and Asia- Pacific Studies.

Mullins, Mark R. (1998) *Christianity Made in Japan: A Study of Indigenous Movements*. Honolulu: University of Hawaii Press.

Mullins, Mark R. (1998) "The Social and Legal Status of Religious Minorities in Japan" paper presented at International Coalition for Religious Freedom Conference on "Religious Freedom and the New Millenium", Tokyo, Louisiana, May 23–25, 1998.

Mullins, Mark R. (2007) "Christianity as a Transnational Social Movement: Kagawa Toyohiko and the Friends of Jesus," *Japanese Religions,* Vol. 32, No. 1.

Nakane, Chie (1973) *Japanese Society*. California: University of California Press.

Naofusa, Hirai (1987) Shinto in Eliade Micrea (ed.), *The Encyclopedia of Religion*. New York: Macmillan Publishing Co.

Napier, Susan J. (1996). *The Fantastic in Modern Japanese Literature: The Subversion of Modernity.* London: Routledge.

Nishiyama, Sekiji (1911) "The Christian Contribution to Japanese Education." The Open Court: Vol. 1911: Issue. 7, Article 6.

Perkin, Harold (1996). *The Third Revolution: Professional Elites in the Modern World.* New York: Routledge.

Rohlen, Thomas P. (1974) *For Harmony and Strength: Japanese White-color Organization in Anthropological Perspective.* Berkley: University of California Press.

Reischauer, Edwin O. (1988). *The Japanese Today: Change and Continuity.* Cambridge: The Belknap Press of Harvard University Press.

Reischauer, Edwin O. and Craig, Albert M. (1989) *Japan: Tradition and Transformation.* Rutland: Vermont and Tokyo.

Storm, Stephanie (2000) "Japan Slowly Embraces Greater Income Inequality over Social Harmony" in New York Times, January 4.

Sugimoto, Yoshio (2003) *An Introduction to Japanese Society.* Cambridge: Cambridge University Press.

Sugimoto, Yoshio (2009) *A Cambridge Companion to Modern Japanese Culture.* Cambridge: Cambridge University Press.

Tadako, Kaname (1991) "Japanese Christian Writers," in *Christianity in Japan*, 1971–90, eds. Kumazawa Yoshinobu & David L. Swain. Tokyo: Kyo Bun Kwan aka The Christian Literature Society of Japan.

Takimoto, Jun (2005) *The Day the Lord Arose.* Shinshiro: All Revival Mission.

Thang, Leng Leng (2002) "Touching of the Hearts: An Overview of Programs to Promote Interaction Between the Generations in Japan" in R. Goodman (ed.), *Family and Social Policy in Japan: Anthropological Approaches.* Cambridge: Cambridge University Press.

Thomsen, Harry (1963) *New Religions of Japan.* Rutland: Charles E. Tuttle.

Relevant Websites

Asian Access Japan
www.asianaccess.org

Christian Examiner
www.christianexaminer.com

Contemporary Japan
http://afe.easia.columbia.edu/at_japan_soc/common/all.htm

CRASH Japan
www.crashjapan.com

Gospel Japan
www.gospeljapan.com

Israelites Came To Japan
http://www5.ocn.ne.jp/~magi9/isracam2.htm

Japan Focus
www.japanfocus.org

Japan Guide Online Resources
www.japan-guide.com

Japan Evangelical Missionary Alliance
www.jema.org

Keikyo the Japan
www.keikyo.com

Ministry of Internal Affairs and Communications
http://www.soumu.go.jp/english/index.html

Mission Japan
www.missionjapan.com

Project Japan
www.projectjapan.org

Reaching Japanese for Christ
www.rjcnetwork.org

Web Japan
http://web-japan.org

ti

www.ingramcontent.com/pod-product-compliance
Lightning Source LLC
Chambersburg PA
CBHW052001090426
42741CB00008B/1493